THE MOST
EXCELLENT WAY

Overcoming Chronic Issues
That Divide the Church

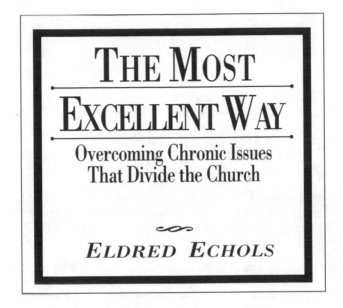

THE MOST EXCELLENT WAY

Overcoming Chronic Issues That Divide the Church

ELDRED ECHOLS

— *A* —
FAITH*FOCUS*
Book

Sweet Publishing

Fort Worth, Texas

The Most Excellent Way
Overcoming Chronic Issues That Divide the Church

Copyright © 1994 by Sweet Publishing
Fort Worth, TX 76137

Cover: Gary Schecter for the Mustang Group

Library of Congress Catalog Number 93-86981

ISBN: 0-8344-0233-5

Printed in the U. S. A.
10 9 8 7 6 5 4 3 2 1

This volume is dedicated to all those throughout the gospel age who have loved the souls of men enough to leave homes and families in order to carry the message of light to those who had never experienced the saving grace of God.

Contents

1 Corinthians 1:1-3, 10

Paul, called to be an apostle of Christ Jesus by the will of God, and our brother Sosthenes,

To the church of God in Corinth, to those sanctified in Christ Jesus and called to be holy, together with all those everywhere who call on the name of our Lord Jesus Christ—their Lord and ours:

Grace and peace to you from God our Father and the Lord Jesus Christ.

I appeal to you, brothers, in the name of our Lord Jesus Christ, that all of you agree with one another so that there may be no divisions among you and that you may be perfectly united in mind and thought.

Chapter 1

Myth of the
Instant Church

1 Corinthians 1:1-17

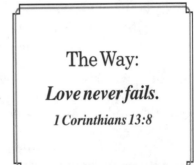

The Way:

Love never fails.

1 Corinthians 13:8

Ephesus, A.D. 55. Fading day watched the tired sun cast orange rays across glistening Asiatic waters as Paul stared out his west window. Lifting his sad eyes across the darkening sea, he tried to recall details of the faces he loved at Corinth, the great city out of sight, on the opposite shore. Tears crept down the leathery cheeks of the apostle as he thought of his beloved children in the faith. They were in trouble—spiritual trouble.

Studying again the letter that had arrived by ship earlier in the day from the Corinthian church, he considered the root problem that had spawned the ugly monsters attacking the struggling church. The answer was obvious. They had lost their true love for one another and for God. They needed to reclaim the family loyalty and caring they had inherited from the Father. They needed to embrace once again their devotion to Jesus and receive his power to overcome their divisions. They needed to set aside selfish ambition, cultural differences, and a history of confrontation in order to be a united family—God's family, the church.

A tear dripped onto the letter, blurring some of the writing. Paul lit the oil lamp and picked up his well-worn quill pen to begin his letter of love to the Christians at Corinth. Somehow he had to help them understand that all their problems could be solved with God's love.

Paul begs the Corinthians in the name of Jesus to agree with each other and be joined completely, having the same thinking and purpose so that they would not be divided. The potential for division in the Corinthian church was inherent in its makeup. Not only was it a blend of two cultures, it was in its beginning a basically Jewish cultural institution that Gentiles and pagans had been brought into. Both cultures, Jewish and Greek, had their own practices and ways of thinking which were causing conflict. Paul knew that they could not be effective if there were divisions and a lack of love among them (1 Corinthians 1:10).

What Is a Church?

Before we can know if a church is unified or divided, we must first know what a church is. The church, like human beings, exists in two dimensions. First and foremost, it is a spiritual kingdom. It is made up of "the firstborn [that is, the heirs of the Father] whose names are written in heaven" (Hebrews 12:23). Only God knows its precise membership. It is the fulfillment of God's eternal purpose in history for the salvation of mankind, and it makes up the one body. The church consists of those who possess God's Spirit and who have submitted to the one Lord, accepted the one faith, and been born again through the one baptism. The church is a theocracy, or divine monarchy, and is undenominational (that is, it has no particular distinguishing name), although it is referred to in several descriptive phrases in the New Testament. It is perfect through the atoning blood of Jesus Christ, "a radiant church, without stain or wrinkle or any other blemish, but holy and blameless" (Ephesians 5:27).

It's unrealistic to think on the day of Pentecost an instant church suddenly sprang into existence on the day the first three thousand Jews were baptized.

The church also exists as a corporate fellowship in local congregations. Its membership is made up of both "wheat and weeds"—both good and bad—and will continue to embrace these different elements until the end of the age (Matthew 13:24-30). Human limitations will prevent it from ever measuring up to its professed ideals. The church's structure of government is essentially democratic, performing its corporate activities under the leadership of overseers chosen by the members.

The church in its identity as a spiritual kingdom came into existence at a precise point in history—the first Pentecost after Jesus' resurrection with the coming of the Holy Spirit. The corporate fellowship already existed in the long-established structures in Judaism, the synagogue in particular. It's unrealistic to think on the day of Pentecost an instant church—

local assemblies of Christians, with responsible leaders, an established pattern of public worship, and functional ministries—suddenly sprang into existence on the day the first three thousand Jews were baptized. As Jews, the people already belonged to local congregations and most were looking for their Messiah.

The identification of Jesus of Nazareth as the Messiah by some Jews would later force a split between their movement and greater Judaism, but in the beginning they were simply "Jews for Jesus," members of local Jewish communities (synagogues), loyal to the temple worship, and "zealous for the Law" (of Moses). They shared with other Jews the attendance at principal feasts (Acts 20:16), regular devotions at the temple (Acts 2:46; 3:1), and obedience to the Law. As practicing Jews, they were already religiously organized. The temple represented the formal Jewish religion and stood as the symbol of their national monotheism (belief in one God). However, their personal and practical religious and social life was centered in the synagogue. Belief in Jesus as the Messiah did not change that, nor would they have anticipated changing it.

The early Christian community did not evolve from the synagogue; it was *the synagogue.*

The early Christian community did not evolve from the synagogue; it *was* the synagogue. When the parting of the ways for Christian Jews and non-Christian Jews eventually came, the Christians took the synagogue with them. Before there was a recognized break between the synagogues of Christians and the synagogues of the unbelieving Jews, Christians began having their own special fellowship gatherings from house to house where they affirmed their new faith in Christ to each other and commemorated his death and resurrection in the breaking of bread. Since from very early times they took the Lord's Supper on the first day of the week, such special assemblies would not have conflicted with their customary participation in the worship of their respective synagogues on the Sabbath. When the break came between the followers of the Way and the synagogues of their parent religion, the separation was at the insistence of the Jews and not the Christians themselves, just as Jesus had said it would happen: "They will put you out of the synagogue" (John 16:2).

Since Christianity became a powerful movement very quickly (historians estimate that within a few months after Pentecost the number of Christians in Jerusalem exceeded thirty thousand), it must have inevitably happened that some synagogues would have been converted as a group to the new faith. In that case they would already have been organized and had a customary pattern of worship and program of community activity. It was simply a matter of adding three dynamic new elements to their families' models: the glorious gospel message of the death, burial, and resurrection of Jesus, the teaching ministry of the apostles, and the indwelling of the Holy Spirit.

The Jewish Christian community during the period of A.D. 29 until the destruction of the temple in A.D. 70 did not regard themselves as organically separate from the Jewish community as a whole, at least as far as Palestine itself was concerned. After all, there were many differing groups in Judaism, such as Essenes, Herodians, Pharisees, Sadducees, Libertines, Alexandrians, etc. who maintained congregations separate from the others, but who regarded themselves as belonging to the greater community of Judaism (Acts 21:17-24). So, these Christians were regarded by the Jews worldwide as simply a troublesome sect of their own community (Acts 24:5, 6; 28:27). That they met for regular services as a special group of Jews who were followers of Jesus of Nazareth would have been taken as a matter of course.

In order to understand the pattern of the earliest Christian assemblies, we must go to the first-century Jewish synagogues for our source.

There is no basic difference in the word translated "church" in the New Testament (*ecclesia*) and the word *synagogue*. Both mean assembly or congregation. Jesus uses the word *ecclesia* in Matthew 18:17 in referring to the synagogue. *Ecclesia* is used almost 100 times in the Greek Old Testament in referring to Hebrew assemblies. So it is completely mistaken that *ecclesia* is a special word used only for Christ's church.

Some Greek-speaking Jews, in fact, used the name *ecclesia* for their congregations, just as early Christians used both names. After the church was well-established among the Gentiles, it became common practice to distinguish between Christians and Jews by using *ecclesia* and *synagogue* separately. It is significant that the English word *church* does not derive from either word, but from *kuriake* (belonging to the Lord).

In order to understand the pattern of the earliest Christian assemblies, we must go to the first-century Jewish synagogues for our source. By studying their

assemblies' organization, structure, and worship, we
are able to better understand the background of the
New Testament itself and, in particular, Paul's first
letter to the Corinthians.

The Synagogue

The synagogue is the oldest continuous religious
institution on earth and is at least twenty-five
hundred years old. Its origin is lost in antiquity, but
most Jewish scholars agree that it began during the
Babylonian exile under the leadership of the prophet
Ezekiel. The oldest evidence of a synagogue in
Jerusalem is an ostracon, or pottery fragment,
owned by W. F. Albright which reads "The House of
the Congregation in Jerusalem" _(Bet Kenisa bi
Yrushalayim)_, dating from the sixth century B.C.

In response to the need of the Jews to remain
faithful to God while in exile (and because they no
longer had access to the temple) the Jews laid the
foundations of what was to become the strongest
influence in Judaism. In Babylon Ezekiel held
teaching sessions, first with the elders in his house
(Ezekiel 8:10) and later with the people (24:18, 19).
They grew into a simple teaching and worship
service, which in time was called a house of instruction _(beth midrash)_, the earliest designation for the
synagogue. These Jewish exiles, cut off from Jerusalem, its temple, and its priesthood, made the synagogue the center of their religious life. By the first
century A.D. it was of much greater relevance for all
Jews, and especially for those communities scattered
throughout the world, than the temple was or ever
could be.

Synagogue worship was more appealing than
temple worship to the common people. They could
participate in its worship services (reading the

Torah[1], reciting prayers, singing hymns together, and joining in responses) and were involved in every aspect of its activity. It did not inspire them with the awe that the spectacle of temple ritual commanded, but it controlled their hearts and lives because they could relate to it personally. The synagogue was much more than congregational ritual. Its ministries addressed virtually every area of Jewish life.

Also, the temple was remote to most Jews living throughout the world, whereas the synagogue was the center of each community. By the time of Jesus, there were synagogues wherever there were Jews. Philo of Alexandria, the Jewish philosopher and historian who was contemporary with Jesus, tells us there were many synagogues in his home city. And, according to the Jerusalem Talmud[2], there were four hundred eighty synagogues in Jerusalem when it was destroyed in A.D. 70.

Functions of the Synagogue

The synagogue was the center of Jewish life. It represented a holistic approach to community life, and that explains both its survival to the present time and its strong hold on the average Jew. According to the *Encyclopedia Judaica,* "From the beginning the Jewish community held nothing human to be beyond its ken. Total care had to be taken of the community, especially the less fortunate members."

Although the synagogue was essentially a community of people, it became common practice to refer to the structure itself as the synagogue (as later happened in the assemblies of Christians). In Hebrew, at different periods and places, it was called House of Assembly (*Beth Ha-Knesset*), House of Reading (*Beth Mikreh)*, and the original name House of Instruction (*Beth Midrash*). In Aramaic it was called the *Kenisa* (Assembly). Philo, Jewish philosopher from Alexandria, referred to the synagogues in Egypt as "houses of prayer." All these titles serve to illustrate the principal functions of the synagogue.

The synagogue was a school. The Talmud required the education of children from the age of six or seven. Each Jewish congregation educated its own children. Philo tells us the synagogues were houses of instruction, "where the philosophy of the fathers and all manner of virtues were taught." At first these programs of education were primarily Scripture classes. But as time progressed they grew into primary and secondary curricula, providing a general education in all aspects of Jewish culture and activity. The teachers, called *tanna* (teacher) or *rabbi* (master) became honored members of the community.

The synagogue was a guest house. The Talmud stated that wayfarers "eat, drink, and sleep in the synagogue." Ruins of ancient synagogues have shown hospitality rooms furnished with provisions for food and lodging. An inscription from an ancient synagogue found on Mt. Ophel, southwest of Jerusalem, mentions "the guest house and the rooms and the supplies of water as an inn for those who are in need when coming from abroad."

The synagogue was the social center for the Jewish community. Not only were celebrations and special occasions observed in the synagogues, but all ages could meet there to enjoy social fellowship. During the period of Greek dominance of Palestine and later in Roman times, the influence of Gentile culture with its public dramas, music, and sports was so pervasive that the Jewish communities were in serious danger of losing their young people. To combat the pull of the world, they planned social

activities for their children and youth which were
centered in the synagogue. One leading rabbi expressed the view that the activity program of the
synagogue should be such that every Jew would
want to spend all of his leisure time there.

*The synagogue was the center of ministries for the
sick, the needy, the orphans, and the elderly.* Members in good standing of a Jewish synagogue were
part of a social security system that addressed every
emergency that might arise in their lives. And when
death came, they had the assurance that their
orphaned children and elderly parents would be
cared for. Ministry to the sick always had been an
important part of Judaism. Jewish congregations
often had physicians as ministers serving their
community who received a basic salary for attending
the poor free of charge. More affluent members were
charged according to their ability to pay. Special
women were trained as nurses and midwives. The
more prosperous members were cared for in their
homes, but the poor were treated in the synagogue
guest house. This ministry gradually grew into the
Jewish hospitals of today. The Talmud also tells us
that a collection was taken at the service. This was
to be done by at least two people (counting the
collection) and distributed by at least three (benevolence ministry). We know that the early church did
exactly the same and probably accounts for Paul's
stipulating hospitality as a requirement for an
enrolled (*catalogued*) widow (1 Timothy 5:10).

The synagogue was a court of justice. Troubles
and strife arising within the synagogue membership
were settled by the community itself and not taken
before Roman magistrates. This protected them from
hostile Gentile courts which had no knowledge of
Hebrew culture and customs. Paul was accustomed

to litigation being handled in-house, and he was shocked that the Corinthian Christians were taking each other to Roman courts. The Talmud required that a synagogue court consist of at least three elders. These courts still exist in every major Jewish settlement and are called rabbinical courts. They have legal force where both parties are in agreement on their jurisdiction. This shows just how far we have departed from the ancient pattern.

The synagogue was a place of worship. Georg Fohrer states: "In it the people assembled for a simple form of worship that consisted of prayers, hymns, and a lecture." (*History of the Israelite Religion*, p. 311.) At first, services appear to have been held only on Sabbaths and feast days, and public reading of the Law was the primary purpose of the service. Since the average Jew could understand only a smattering of Hebrew, the reading was translated into Aramaic. This translation called the Targum grew into an explanation, and the explanation into an exposition with an application, much like the organization of a modern sermon. When Paul wrote to Timothy to "devote yourself to the public reading of Scripture, to preaching and to teaching" (1 Timothy 4:13), that is what he was referring to. However, the oratorical homily, a sermon that cannot be interrupted, developed from Greek rhetoric. This is the pattern we follow today in our worship services. The rabbinical style of preaching was more like our Bible classes. The subject was introduced by the speaker, but members of the audience could challenge him on points or ask questions. Apparently this is what was happening in Corinth (1 Corinthians 14).

In addition to its special functions as a school, a hotel, a community center, a hospital, a law court, and a house of worship, the synagogue gave to each member the sense of personal identity and standing in a group where he had value and recognition. It was a lifestyle that made life meaningful and precious.

The synagogue was a bright example of caring in an uncaring, heathen world. The Christians built upon the synagogue's foundation of love for its members and were led beyond it. Our Savior's supreme example of selfless, unfailing love, gave new definition to love in the first-century world. The Christians' love for each other and for all people made them lighthouses in the darkness of paganism.

The Corinthian church was divided because it had lost the spirit, community, and love of its godly heritage—the heritage of the synagogue, predecessor of Christ's church. To say that division still exists in today's church is an understatement. We understand that God is love and that we are to share his love with those around us, especially fellow Christians. But it is with our own family of believers that we often have the greatest conflict. Too many times our conflicts are over minor issues that have no clear biblical precedent or command as their basis. But because of our previous teachings and traditions we take positions for or against the issues and have little or no tolerance for opposing views. Sometimes a simple understanding of the origin of our long accepted traditions helps us to consider other views. Sometimes knowing the historical or cultural context of a passage makes the issues clearer.

This study will raise questions which people may accept in different ways. But we must not let our differences cause us to be divided. We can have unity if we concentrate on the message of love in Paul's letter to the Corinthian church. Let us pray for understanding through the Holy Spirit so that we

can honestly examine our hearts and better apply
Paul's teachings.

Notes:

[1] Torah—the Pentateuch, or Five Books of Moses, that
contains the Jewish law.

[2] Talmud—the Hebrew book of instruction which contains
the rabbinical laws, law decisions, and commentary on the
laws of Moses.

Focusing Your Faith

1. How does your church resemble a synagogue?

2. In what ways does your church function like a guest house? A hospital? A court? A school? A social center?

3. The synagogue was called by various names (House of Instruction, Assembly, etc.). If your congregation were named according to what takes place there, what would it be called?

4. What do you consider the primary function of the church today?

5. Since the synagogue was developed by people to address a need rather than by God's command, was it a good pattern for the early church to imitate?

6. How can churches today provide opportunity for the intimate, personal relationships that the small home church once did?

7. If you were to organize your church service like that of the synagogue-church's, what would it be like? What objections would you expect to hear? What compliments?

1 Corinthians 1:11, 12; 16:15, 16

*My brothers, some from Chloe's house-
hold have informed me that there are
quarrels among you. What I mean is this:
One of you says, "I follow Paul"; another, "I
follow Apollos"; another, "I follow Cephas";
still another, "I follow Christ."*

*You know that the household of
Stephanas were the first converts in Achaia,
and they have devoted themselves to the
service of the saints. I urge you, brothers, to
submit to such as these and to everyone who
joins in the work, and labors at it.*

Chapter 2

Lead, Serve, or Get Out of the Way

1 Corinthians 1:11, 12; 3:1-9; 16:15, 16

Alexander the Great was a small man scarcely five feet in height, yet he commanded great armies of loyal troops who would follow him anywhere. One of the reasons he was a great leader was that he cared deeply about his soldiers. On his return march from his Indian campaign, he had to march his army through the harsh Makran desert of Pakistan. Previously, Cyrus the Persian and the Pharaoh Semiramis had lost armies from hunger and thirst in trying to cross that same desert. As Alexander and his men raced against time and death to cross that dismal tract, their water gave out. Just enough water was found for Alexander himself, and it was brought to him.

> **The Way:**
>
> *Love rejoices with the truth.*
>
> *1 Corinthians 13:6*

Through cracked lips he said, "There is not enough to share, so I will not drink alone. I am not thirsty for myself, I am thirsty for my whole army." And so, like David at the cave of Adullam (2 Samuel 23:17), he refused to drink the water, pouring it out upon the ground.

Another remarkable story comes from a war between Denmark and Sweden in the 1660s. After a savage battle (which Denmark won) an ordinary Danish soldier took his canteen and was about to drink when he heard a cry for water from a wounded Swede a short distance away. The Dane went to the man and said, "Your need is greater than mine." But while he was putting his flask to the wounded soldier's lips, the Swede pulled a pistol from his jacket and shot the Dane in the shoulder. The Danish soldier exclaimed, "You rascal: I befriended you and you tried to kill me. Now I am going to punish you. I had intended giving you the whole flask of water, but now you will get only half." Having said that, the Dane then drank half the bottle and gave the rest to the Swede. When this was reported to the Danish king, Fredrick, the monarch immediately summoned the soldier and said to him, "You have the quality to become a great leader," and he made the man a noble on the spot.

Leaders in God's Service

One of the more glaring deficiencies of the church at Corinth was its lack of effective leadership. There was no cohesion in the congregation and no common purpose. Apparently, the Corinthians were reluctant to follow the leadership of people from within their congregation who had given themselves to God's service. This is surprising in view of the fact that a primary cause of division in the congregation was their eagerness to follow certain influential evangelists: Peter (Cephas), Paul, and Apollos. The Corinthians were divided into these affinity groups and were taking pride in their differences rather than seeking unity. They had no recognized overseers to arbitrate wrongs in the group, with the result that any decisions had to be made by the corporate assembly. Since immature and unspiritual people made up the majority of the church, the practical result was that "even men of little account in the church" were sitting in judgment over matters in which they had no competence. Paul was unaccustomed to this type of reckless open democracy of the Greeks because he had grown up in the institutions of Judaism. And it was the Jewish synagogue leadership style that Paul used as a model for New Testament leadership.

Synagogue Leadership

Every fully organized synagogue was under the supervision of mature and respected elders (Luke 7:3-5). These elders were elected by the people themselves for their wisdom and experience. The Hebrews had always had elders over their communities and nation at every level. They were already in existence when Moses began his special ministry to Israel. The elders were not primarily over the services and functions of the synagogue itself but rather over the community of people. In other words, they were not directly involved in the running of the synagogue. Nevertheless, major decisions could not be made without their approval. For instance, the Talmud states that a synagogue may not be sold to be used for any other purpose than that for which it was built without the approval of the elders.

Mark 5:22 and Acts 13:15 record that there were certain "synagogue rulers." Scholars believe they were chosen from among the elders. The actual direction of the synagogue service was entrusted to "leaders of the synagogue" ("rulers" of the synagogue is not a desirable translation). They had charge of the service and decided who was to speak and lead prayers. These were referred to under two titles: (1) the Announcer of the Congregation (*Hazzan Ha-Knesset*) and (2) the Messenger of the Community (*Sheli'ach zibbur*). The announcer was in charge of the service with the special duty of leading the songs and chants. In later times he became the *cantor* and was the counterpart of the song leader in Christian services. In responsorial singing he sang the lead, and the congregation sang the response. The messenger led in the readings from the Torah, the ritual prayers, and often the hymns. His successor in the Christian organization of services would possibly be the prophet of the first century and early second century and the preacher of later times.

The announcer and the messenger had the option of speaking to the assembly or finding someone else to do it. The same applied to reading the Scriptures, leading in prayers, and so on. The public discourse was made up of explanation of the reading for the day and encouragement. That is the background of Acts 13:15. After the scroll was read, the leaders of the assembly invited Paul and his companions: "Brothers, if you have a message of encouragement for the people, please speak." The announcer had to take responsibility for what his guest speaker said, and if the message was too outrageous the announcer might be publicly flogged, as happened to Sosthenes at Corinth (Acts 18:17). In later times the public preacher of a synagogue was called the *rabbi*;

however, in New Testament times *rabbis* were not a part of the synagogue organization.

In addition to these jobs, there were special ministers of the synagogue who were called *huperetai* (literally, "under-rowers" or servants). This office is mentioned in Luke 4:20 on the occasion where Jesus read the Scripture in the synagogue in Nazareth: "Then he rolled up the scroll, gave it back to the attendant [KJV "minister"] and sat down." These attendants or servants may have been the same as the men of the synagogue called in Hebrew *parnasim* (literally, "providers of food") who were in charge of the benevolence ministry. If that is so, they would have been the forerunners of the Christian deacons.

Jerusalem Church Leadership

In Jewish churches the synagogue organization was simply continued after the congregation became Christians. In Acts 11:30 elders suddenly appear in the text without explanation—a sign that they were an already accepted institution. The context would suggest that they were elders of the Jerusalem congregation(s), but how or when they were installed in their capacity of leadership is not stated. We may assume from Acts 15:2, 4, 6, 22, 23, and 16:4 that they met with the apostles as a decision-making body. In that early period of the Jerusalem church, they are never mentioned as functioning separately from the apostles. By the time of Paul's final visit to Jerusalem, however, the transition appears to have been made from an apostle-elder oversight of the church to an oversight by the elders alone (Acts 21:8).

The early leadership of the Jerusalem church was vested in the apostles (Acts 4:37; 6:2). A problem arose when it became apparent that they were expected to take immediate responsibility in areas not directly related to their spiritual ministry. They proposed that a panel of seven men should be chosen by the congregation to oversee benevolence so that they themselves would not have to serve (*diakonein*) tables. Possibly because they used the word *deacon* in referring to the responsibility or because of the nature of the work itself, these men were regarded by succeeding generations of Christians as the first deacons, and, indeed, logically so. The procedure employed in establishing them in office follows:[1]

- First, they were chosen by the congregation (not by the apostles) according to guidelines laid down by the apostles.

- Secondly, they were *appointed* (ordained, set in office) by the apostles with prayer and the laying on of hands.

"Submit to Such as These"

Paul's language in pleading with the Corinthians to submit to leaders brings up some interesting points: "I urge you, brothers to submit to such as these and to everyone who joins in the work and labors at it" (1 Corinthians 16:15, 16). Why didn't he, as an apostle, simply command them to choose leaders? There are probably several reasons, among which may be:

1. It was not the practice of the apostles to impose leadership upon congregations. The admonition of the apostles to the Jerusalem church to choose special servants arose out of a complaint from the members that the relief effort was poorly organized. The apostles made sure that those selected were the choices of the people.

2. Imposed leadership that does not take into account the will of the people sows the seed of rebellion, not of harmony. Leaders cannot lead unless people are willing to follow them.

3. Unrestrained leadership tends to _rule_ rather than to _lead_ by example. For instance, Peter warned against elders "lording it over" those who were entrusted to them. The notion of _ruling_ is largely attributable to the King James Version's translation of the word _lead_ in 1 Timothy 3:4, 5; 5:17 and _leaders_ in Hebrews 13:17. (The folly of a _ruler_ in a church is well-illustrated by the example of Diotrephes in 3 John 9, 10.)

Spiritual Qualifications of Leaders

There is a strong implication that Paul would have liked to see the Corinthians choose (among others) certain members of the Stephanas family as leaders of the church. He, nevertheless, does not go so far as to actually nominate them but uses them as examples of the kind of leaders to look for: "submit to such as these." He gives as qualifying factors:

1. They were the first converts (experienced).

2. They had devoted themselves to the service of the saints.

Paul adds that whomever they choose should be Christians who have really applied themselves to the work of the church. Even in the case of the special servants chosen in Acts 6, the apostles required that they be "known to be full of the Spirit and wisdom." Paul wrote of certain Christians at Corinth that they had "devoted themselves to the service of the saints." He knew that great leaders are primarily concerned about the welfare of their followers. They rejoice in the truth of the gospel, and

like shepherds, they are willing to sacrifice themselves for their sheep (John 10:11).

Elders

Spiritual leaders strive to keep their flock's focus
on the gospel of Christ. Elders are men who love
their church and want the best possible for them—
both for this life and for eternity. Unfortunately,
today's shepherds often serve as a managing board
of directors or a panel of financial controllers as well.

We have too often concentrated upon easily
determined physical qualifications for elders (based
upon the lists of guidelines given in 1 Timothy 3 and
Titus 1) and ignored the far more important spiritual qualifications that really determine whether a
man is elder material. The result has been that men
have been selected because they had a wife and two
children who had been immersed (although often
they were not dedicated Christians), but they lacked
the wisdom and spiritual stature to serve as shepherds.

The application of many of the guidelines in the
pastoral epistles is, at best, a highly subjective
exercise, since applying these guidelines depends
largely upon one's perception. A man who is regarded as an able teacher in one setting is quite
inadequate in another. What is a recent convert? A
Christian for six months? Two years? How many
degrees are there between gentle and quarrelsome?
If he rates six on a scale of one to ten, is he acceptable? What about qualities not listed, like *wise,
generous,* and *patient*? Are they necessary? Whether
or not a man meets all the points on a checklist, he
must certainly be evaluated on two basic questions:
(1) Will he serve effectively as an elder? and (2) Will

he be accepted as an elder?

Selection of Elders

The first recorded selection of elders in the Gentile churches appears in Acts 14:23. There seems to
be an incongruity in language here because the very
word used for the selection (*cheirotoneo*) denotes to
elect by a show of hands, but the subject of the verb
appears to be Paul and Barnabas. This has been
taken to indicate that the two evangelists chose
elders for the various churches. This tension is
reflected in various Greek-English lexicons where
the normal meaning of *to vote by the raising of the
hand* is given first, and then (on the basis of Acts
14:23) a secondary meaning of *appoint* is given.

Adam Clarke, the well-known Wesleyan wrote:
"But what is the meaning of the word . . . which we
translate *ordained*: (It) signifies the holding up or
stretching out the hand, as approving the choice of
any person to a particular work."

The Byzantine church historian John Zonaras
said: "Anciently, the choice or suffrage [vote] was
called *cheirotonia* [the noun form of *cheirotoneo*], for
when it was lawful for the multitude in their cities
to choose their priests and bishops, they met together, and some chose one man, some another; but
that it might appear whose suffrage won, they say
the electors used to stretch forth their hands, and by
their hands so stretched forth, or up, they were
numbered who chose the one and who the other."

As a matter of history, this practice was continued down to the eleventh century, and when the
right of the people to elect their own bishops was
taken away there was rioting in the streets of Milan.
The prominent Lutheran scholar, Richard Lenski,
translated Acts 14:23: "Moreover, after the vote

appointing for them elders from church to church, by praying after fasting, they commended them to the Lord in whom they had believed." He comments on the passage: "As in 2 Corinthians 8:19, *cheirotoneo* means to vote by stretching out the hand." The NIV makes the marginal note on Acts 14:23: "or . . . ordained elders or . . . had elders elected." But it is not necessary to belabor the point. The evidence is overwhelming that Paul used exactly the same procedure in having elders elected as was used to choose deacons in Acts 6. Nor is Titus 1:5 an exception as has sometimes been suggested. It is referring to the actual installation of the elected elders. The word translated "appoint" is *kathistemi* which means to set in office according to some system of guidelines.

After the people had expressed their preference, the evangelist made sure that the nominees were suitable men before they formally ordained them.

Paul lists some qualities desirable in men who are to serve as elders in Titus 1:6-9 and 1 Timothy 3:1-7. Titus and Timothy, the evangelists, were to make sure the choices of the congregation were qualified men before they laid hands on them. He particularly warns Timothy: "Do not lay hands upon anyone too hastily and thus share responsibility for the sins of others" (1 Timothy 5:22). After the people had expressed their preference, the evangelist made sure that the nominees were suitable men before they formally ordained them. This corresponds to what happened in Acts 14:23. The congregation selected the men they were willing to submit to; then a period of prayer and fasting followed, and finally the evangelists "presented" (*paratithemi*) them to the Lord (publicly ordained them).

This method of selecting elders continued beyond the New Testament period. We know from a letter written to the Corinthian church by Clement of Rome in about A.D. 95 that Corinth had finally heeded Paul's advice to appoint leaders. Unfortunately, they later changed their minds and put them out of office. Clement's letter expresses outrage, not because they had expelled the elders from office per se, but because they had done it without just cause. He wrote: "We consider therefore that it is not just to remove from their ministry those who were appointed by them [apostles], or later on by other eminent men, with the consent of the whole church, and have ministered to the flock of Christ without blame, humbly, peaceably, and disinterestedly, and for many years have received a universally favorable testimony."

This quote from Clement's Corinthian epistle brings out two interesting facts. The first is that elders were installed by eminent men (evangelists in the context) with the consent of the church itself. The obvious inference is that the will of the congregation was first obtained by some form of voting, after which the elders selected were ordained by acknowledged evangelists.

One of the earliest post-New Testament documents written is the *Didache* (or the *Teachings of the Twelve Apostles*). It dates from no later than A.D. 115 and is almost as early as Clement's letter. The author is unknown, but the writing was accepted in the second-century church. It states regarding the selection of elders: "Elect therefore for yourselves bishops and deacons worthy of the Lord, meek men, and not lovers of money, and truthful and proved."

This shows that:

1. Congregations still elected their elders and deacons in the second century.
2. There was still a plurality of elders in every church.
3. Congregations were only entitled to elect men who were qualified (worthy of the Lord).

This procedure endured for a surprisingly long time. According to Philip Schaff[2] "The Greek church, after the eighth century, vested the franchise exclusively in the bishops (Council of Nice, A.D. 787). The Latin church, after the eleventh century, vested it in the clergy of the cathedral church." In other words, bishops appointed bishops, with the result that the New Testament system of checks and balances was circumvented. The result was the bishops became increasingly arrogant and autocratic, and the people had no way of correcting the situation.

Checks and Balances

In New Testament times the evangelist was charged with the responsibility of rebuking an elder who violated his position of trust (1 Timothy 5:19, 20). The fact that he was able to do so suggests that his livelihood was not as dependent upon the good will of the elders as is the case of a congregational minister today. It is likely that he was engaged and dismissed by both congregation and elders and not by either acting alone.

The importance of the evangelist both in serving as a check against the congregation's choosing popular but unqualified men, and against an elder's abusing his position of power, has been largely lost in the church today because of the evangelist's financial dependence. Timothy and Titus (and no doubt many

others mentioned in the New Testament) were the
generation of evangelists who succeeded to that
public ministry of the Word first performed by the
apostles. They were "your leaders, who spoke the
word of God to you" (Hebrew 13:7). That explains
why the qualifications of elders were written to
Timothy and Titus (evangelists), rather than to
congregations, because these evangelists were not to
hastily ordain men chosen by congregations until
they had verified that they possessed the required
qualities. This served the purpose of protecting the
people against themselves (when they chose unsuit-
able men) and against episcopal (elder) ordination
(since elders, or bishops, would tend to ordain men
who supported them in whatever biases they might
have). The removal of the evangelist from the divine
system of checks and balances was an early and
basic departure from the New Testament organization and resulted in the development of the ecclesiastical power structure which destroyed primitive
Christianity. By the beginning of the third century
the evangelist of the first century no longer existed,
and the course was inevitably set toward the mon-
strous ecclesiastical power structure that dominated
religious life in both East and West in the post-
Nicene period (the fourth century onward).

Elders Choosing Elders

The selection and installation of elders by the
existing elders is a practice that is filled with peril
and hostile to the spirit of New Testament church
government. As a matter of principle and integrity,
elders should scrupulously avoid any manipulation
or "behind-the-scenes" intervention in the process of
the congregation's choice of the men they want as
leaders. The temptation to intervene is strong, and

many instances of a congregation's "free choice" of their elders is much less than that because existing elders have intervened by deleting names from a secret nomination list. The result is that congregations only exercise their choice in approving men on a list already reduced by the existing elders to names acceptable to them. This is one of the most destructive ways of entrenching a particular doctrinal bias or error in a church, and church history abounds with its tragic consequences.

Do existing elders have the right to voice an objection to the ordination of men who are unqualified to serve as elders? They not only have the right, but the responsibility to do so, as does every other member of the congregation. But objections from elders should be given special weight since they were chosen because of their maturity and leadership.

The ancient axiom, "power corrupts" is much more than just a saying.

The specific mechanics for the nomination of elders where an eldership is not already in existence, or for adding additional elders to an eldership already serving, are not delineated in the New Testament. We do not know the process by which the Jerusalem church was to *seek out* qualified men for special servants, nor do we know how Paul expected the Corinthian church to "submit themselves" to qualified leaders. Acts 14:23 and Titus 1:5 may indicate that evangelists took the initiative in the case of young congregations, the inference being that the evangelist would better understand the qualifications which the candidates would have to meet.

In the case of long-established congregations there should reasonably be teachers, ministers, and other Christians of experience who could organize the nomination and election procedure and judge the merits of objections lodged against the nominees. In such a situation it would not seem to be productive to bring in an outside evangelist as a moderator, since he would not know the congregation like leading members would know it. It should be obvious that existing elders should excuse themselves from active involvement in the process. Paul warned that it would be from among the elders themselves that destructive practices would arise (Acts 20:30), and indeed the very practice of bishops' interfering in the right of the people to choose their own bishops led to the hierarchy which virtually destroyed the church.

In view of this, elders should be extremely conscientious in obeying Paul's exhortation to "Be careful to do what is right in the eyes of everybody." The ancient axiom, "power corrupts" is much more than just a saying. Even the practice of elders appointing a screening committee to supervise the nomination of additional elders is open to abuse and misinterpretation. It is especially ill-advised if there is already some dissatisfaction in the congregation. The often repeated rationale that "we cannot abandon our responsibility to the congregation" is laying claim to one responsibility which the Lord never gave them. It is important, however, that whoever selects a screening committee be perceived by the members as representing the interests of the congregation and as serving as the instruments of the existing eldership.

Ordination of Elders

The actual installation of elders, after the congregation has expressed its choice, has been a touchy point in some churches. The very word *ordain* has stirred emotions. It is a translation of the Greek verb *kathistemi,* which simply means "to appoint to or install in a position according to a set of guidelines." It has already been pointed out that ordination to church offices (special functions) was performed by evangelists in New Testament times (Acts 6:6; 14:23; 1 Timothy 5:22; Titus 1:5). It is described in Acts 14:23 as "presenting them to the Lord," after prayer and fasting. So, the early Christians gave the ceremony a much higher profile than it often gets in our churches today. This is at least partially due to our discomfort with the New Testament practices of fasting and the "laying on" of hands.

Fasting, it is often noted, was never commanded or bound on Christians by the apostles, and that is true enough. It is simply assumed in New Testament references. Jesus, referring to the future period after his return to heaven, said to his followers: "Then shall they fast in those days" (Matthew 9:15; Mark 2:20; Luke 5:35). Paul anticipates Christians' fasting by saying ". . . that ye may give yourselves to prayer and fasting" (KJV—*fasting* is omitted in the NIV and NASB, but occurs in several manuscripts).

Paul himself often fasted (2 Corinthians 6:5; 11:27), and it seems to have been the general practice in a congregation when a momentous event such as appointing elders or sending out missionaries occurred (Acts 13:3; 14:23). Even today there are some congregations who practice fasting before important congregational decisions. And there are many individual Christians who practice it because they believe it to be of benefit in enhancing spiritual awareness and depth of earnestness in prayer. Fasting can be counter-productive if it is conceived to be sacramental or meritorious self-denial.

Laying on of hands has generally been avoided in

many Restoration churches because of the association with two erroneous practices:

1. Laying on of hands has been used to administer priestly functions or to acknowledge "holy orders." What began as a simple ceremony of separation to a special responsibility was perverted by the Old Catholic Church into a *sacrament* separating the clergy from the laity and restricting significant church functions to the clergy.

2. More recently, it has been used by neo-Pentecostals as the "apostolic" means of transmitting the miraculous power of the Spirit, generally in the context of tongue speaking and divine healing.

But the laying on of hands is an ancient biblical practice preceding the Christian era by almost two thousand years. Throughout the Mosaic period, sin offerings and burnt offerings were set apart by the offerer's laying on of hands (Exodus 29:10; Leviticus 1:4; 2 Chronicles 29:23). The other tribes laid their hands upon the tribe of Levi to set them apart for the Lord's service (Numbers 8:10). Moses appointed Joshua his successor with the laying on of hands (Numbers 27:23). For most of biblical history, the significance of laying on of hands was dedication or separation. Its use for imparting charismatic gifts was limited to the brief period of the apostles' ministry (at most 70 years).

Elders for Life?

Finally, what redress has a congregation against elders who are not qualified? Sometimes Acts 20:28 is presented as proof that the Holy Spirit appoints elders to be overseers and that, therefore, their tenure in office is not subject to human termination. This misinterpretation has resulted in split congregations and empty buildings throughout the United States. The Holy Spirit appoints elders through the human means described in the New Testament, and he removes them by the same human means.

When the followers are no longer willing to follow, the leaders no longer lead. If elders were elected for a clearly understood term of office, most of the power struggles which plague the churches would never occur. No honorable man will wish to hold on to a position where he is not wanted or in which his leadership is not respected. No dishonorable man should have that choice. A true leader, a lover of truth, with a servant spirit will welcome an expression of confidence, or lack of it, from the congregation, lest he inadvertently lord it over the flock. A man who lacks the humility to submit his commission of leadership to the will of the congregation is no longer a scriptural elder and is simply holding on to an empty title after its reality is gone.

Leaders rejoice in truth in every aspect of their lives and interpersonal relationships. But moreover, it is a priority that leaders rejoice in the truth of the gospel. They are to be the ones who say, in word and in deed, "I follow Christ."

Notes:

[1] Deaconesses are discussed in the chapter "What About Women."

[2] Philip Schaff, *History of the Christian Church*, Vol. 4, p. 241.

Focusing Your Faith

1. How comfortable would you be with an overseer coming to you to discuss a problem he sees in your life? How would his attitude affect your receptiveness?

2. Each faction at Corinth thought it was more spiritual than the others. How can we avoid that mistake?

3. What three qualities do you think are the most essential for a good leader?

4. How could prayer and fasting be applied in today's church? Laying on of hands?

5. How does submitting to another make you stronger? What position does love have in balancing leadership and submission?

6. What can you do to get to know your leaders better? To let your leaders know you? How can your church help?

7. How comfortable would you be in approaching an elder with a problem? With good news?

1 Corinthians 1:22-24

Jews demand miraculous signs and Greeks look for wisdom, but we preach Christ crucified: a stumbling block to Jews and foolishness to Gentiles, but to those whom God has called, both Jews and Greeks, Christ the power of God and the wisdom of God.

Chapter 3

The Foolishness
of Grace

1 Corinthians 1:18–2:5

The Way:

Love is not proud.

1 Corinthians 13:4

An eighteenth-century British ship was sailing off the coast of South America. The trade winds had been light, prolonging the voyage, and the sailors used up all the ship's drinking water. Eventually, a Spanish galleon sailed into view going in the opposite direction. When the Spaniards were within hailing distance, the English signaled: "Our water is exhausted. Help us." They received the astonishing reply: "Put down your bucket where you are." They were incensed at the impertinence of the answer and sent a more urgent message: "We are dying. Give us water." Again the unbelievable response: "Put down your bucket where you are!" The British officers were stunned at the cruel and uncivil response and exploded in helpless rage. Finally, one officer dared to suggest, "Why don't we try it? It can't hurt, and we have no other solution." Eventually, wise counsel prevailed, and they drew up a bucket of water from the sea and found it salt-free and drinkable. They were in the outgoing flow of the great Amazon River whose mighty volume of water separates the Atlantic for more than a hundred miles from land. The ridiculous suggestion turned out to be the wisest one they had heard for some time.

I wonder how tired the Lord gets of people who write out their own prescriptions for salvation.

Skilled professional people often have to endure free, unsolicited advice from people whose attitudes boast a know-it-all intelligence. Lawyers have their cases preempted by clients. Medical doctors and chiropractors have patients who not only explain in detail their symptoms but also describe the expected treatment. They are offended if their ailment is played down by the practitioner. I once went to a chiropractor after traditional medicine had failed to relieve a chronically painful back. The chiropractor probed a while, then took some x-rays. He was blunt. "I could take your money for a series of adjustments, but there's really nothing wrong with you except that one leg is slightly shorter than the other. If you'll go next door to the pharmacy and buy a heel pad, your pain will go away." I was outraged that he had reduced a serious problem—most likely a spinal tumor—to a fifty-cent heel pad. I, nevertheless, bought one to show the imbecile up for the charlatan he was. The pad worked.

I wonder how tired the Lord gets of people who

write out their own prescriptions for salvation. More likely, it makes him very sad because none of their prescriptions will work. Only the plan that God devised from eternity can take a human soul from the kingdom of Satan into the kingdom of Christ, however foolish it may seem to boasting conventional wisdom.

The Corinthian Christians had no reason to boast about their own part in their salvation. Paul makes it clear that it was because of God that they were in Christ Jesus, not because of their own great wisdom. They had no wisdom to boast of except that of Jesus, the very wisdom from God.

The gospel message of salvation is never preached in a cultural vacuum. There are always prejudices in any society, in any age. Preconceived notions may so screen people's willingness to accept new truths that their hearts become "stony ground" into which the seeds of the gospel cannot penetrate. The New Testament age was no different. Both Jewish and Gentile cultures had erected barriers that blinded them to any challenge to their set modes of thinking.

Jewish Pride

The Jews were a virtually closed religious culture. They had circled their theological wagons and were deaf to any message that did not correspond to their traditional interpretation of Scripture. They had all the truth that they could ever possibly need and were not looking for any more. Their "rightness" was guaranteed by their exclusive position as God's chosen people, so the possibility of their being wrong was unthinkable. They were the only people on earth who truly served God according to his laws, and, therefore, the only people worthy of his favor. Any message that challenged their uniqueness carried the seeds of its own rejection. Most of them had become a "cult" in the sense that only they had a relationship with God, and only they were the recipients and custodians of all truth.

Complicating Truth

There is always a tendency in humanity to complicate simple truths. A world-renowned orchestra director was rehearsing a composition with the London Philharmonic Orchestra. While they were practicing a rendition of the work, he suddenly stopped them in frustration and exclaimed, "You must play this part with more assertiveness and conviction, with deeper feeling and expression." The orchestra members stared at him blankly for a moment, and then one raised his hand. "Maestro," he asked, "do you mean you want us to play it louder?" The great artist didn't respond for a moment, and then he replied meekly, "Yes, that is exactly what I mean."

Theologians have so embellished the simple message of the gospel that they have made the original meaning all but incomprehensible. One has only to open John Calvin's *Institutes* to quickly see that if God depended on learned logicians to explain his terms of pardon to the world, most of us would remain forever in darkness.

One of the reasons Jesus was the master teacher is that he communicated God's love in language and concepts so basic that even the most ignorant peasant could understand it. People have spent two thousand years complicating what was originally a universal gospel into libraries full of volumes on systematic theology.

The Corinthians, in common with the entire

Greek civilization of the Mediterranean world, reverenced knowledge. To them, humans came nearest to grasping the reality of God through abstract reasoning than through any other way. This set the stage for the development of the Gnostic heresy (salvation through knowledge) which plagued the church in the second century. Paul was determined not to fall into the trap of mental games the Corinthians were so fond of playing. The gospel he preached placed no premium on rational skills or intellectual skills; it was designed to move penitent, humble hearts to accept God's loving grace expressed in the crucifixion of Jesus Christ.

Theologians have so embellished the simple message of the gospel that they have made the original meaning all but incomprehensible.

One of history's most bizarre turning points is the rejection by most Jews of the gospel message. The Jewish people were the obvious primary beneficiaries of the promise. To use Paul's words: "Theirs is the adoption as sons; theirs the divine glory, the covenants, the receiving of the law, the temple worship and the promises. Theirs are the patriarchs, and from them is traced the human ancestry of Christ, who is God over all, forever praised! Amen" (Romans 9:4, 5).

During the long period when the rest of the world "neither glorified him as God nor gave thanks to him" (Romans 1:21), the descendants of Jacob held on to the worship of the one true God (with some lapses, to be sure, but they always came back). They have suffered indescribable miseries and persecutions from the time of the Egyptian bondage down to the twentieth century. During much of that time

they have been held together by the Messianic hope
that a Deliverer would come to give them ultimate
victory. What a tragedy beyond expression that
when the Messiah did come, most of them didn't
recognize him! And so the Jews, who still hold onto
the hope of a Messiah's coming, go on waiting for
something to happen that has long since come to
pass.

Stumbling on the Cross

In the words of Paul, "What Israel sought so
earnestly it did not obtain" (Romans 11:7). The cross
proved a stumbling block of such magnitude that it
effectively blocked the entrance to the kingdom to
many Jews. Although the cross was itself the entrance to the kingdom, the Jew saw it as an
unscalable wall instead of as a door. Some of the
reasons Jews had for rejecting the Messiah are the
following:

*1. Jesus did not fit their preconceived image of the
Messiah.* They were looking for a leader who would
provide political solutions to their problems, not
spiritual birth. The Messiah was to be a second
David. But whereas David had reigned over all
Israel "from Dan to Beersheba" (2 Samuel 3:10), the
Messianic king of David's house would rule over the
entire world. "Foreigners will rebuild your walls, /
and their kings will serve you. / . . . For the nation or
kingdom that will not serve you will perish; it will be
utterly ruined" (Isaiah 60:10, 12). The humiliation
they had suffered under a historical pageant of
conquerors, reaching the low point in the irksome
Roman occupation, would be more than avenged.
The Romans would come to Jerusalem to beg for
their mercy: "The sons of your oppressors will come

bowing before you; / all who despise you will bow down at your feet / and will call you the City of the LORD, / Zion of the Holy One of Israel" (v. 14).

Palestine in the first century A.D. was a political powder keg ready to explode. Already two Jewish rebellions under Theudas and Judas the Galilean (Acts 5:35-37) had been ruthlessly suppressed by the Romans. Barabbas had been part of an uprising (Luke 23:19). This smoldering discontent was to break out into open warfare in the Jewish-Roman wars of A.D. 66–70 and again in the Bar-Kokhba rebellion, fifty years later, with devastating results for the Jewish people. Israel was in no mood in the second decade of the first century to accept a Messiah who urged them to pay the Romans' taxes and who declared that his kingdom was of the heart and could not be visually observed (Luke 17:20, 21).

Although the cross was itself the entrance to the kingdom, the Jew saw it as an unscalable wall instead of as a door.

Isaiah had prophesied that the Messiah would be Prince of Peace (9:6), and Zechariah wrote that their king would be "gentle and riding on a donkey" (9:9). Malachi warned them that when the one they were expecting actually came, they would be quite unprepared for him: " 'Then suddenly the Lord you are seeking will come to his temple; the messenger of the covenant, whom you desire, will come,' says the LORD Almighty. But who can endure the day of his coming? Who can stand when he appears? For he will be like a refiner's fire or a launderer's soap" (Malachi 3:1b, 2). They were expecting a Jewish counterpart of Alexander the Great who would sweep the Romans into the sea and restore David's kingdom and increase it to the ends of the earth. The gentle teacher from Nazareth was the epitome of what they were *not* expecting.

2. *The crucifixion was a humiliating defeat.* It was no victory in Jewish eyes. Had not Moses himself said: "Anyone who is hung on a tree is under God's curse" (Deuteronomy 21:23)? How could the Christians preach that such a dismal failure was in reality a glorious triumph? Jesus had not defeated the Roman enemy and restored the kingdom to Israel. He had been executed as a base criminal by the Roman authorities.

3. *The Christian gospel rejected the Jews as God's chosen people.* And it reduced Jews to the same status before God as the unclean nations around them. It was a humiliating affront to their national Jewish pride and dignity that they were now expected to accept as equals the very people they had been required to stay separate from for generations. What about all the promises that they were the special, chosen descendants of Abraham and Jacob (1 Chronicles 16:13; Psalm 105:6)?

4. *This new message taught that circumcision was no longer necessary to be included among God's people.* Even if it was argued that the law given on Sinai was no longer binding, circumcision had been required centuries before Moses, for God had told Abraham, "For the generations to come every male among you who is eight days old must be circumcised. . . . My covenant in your flesh is to be an everlasting covenant" (Genesis 17:12, 13).

5. *The doctrine of salvation by grace alone and justification apart from works provided no incentive for moral integrity.* Instead, it discounted human righteousness as being of no value in alleviating God's judgment. Such a doctrine degraded Israel's

fifteen centuries of law-keeping and exacted no penalty for the Gentiles' past depravities.

Reasons to Believe the Cross

On the other hand, there were compelling reasons why an honest Jew with a reasonable knowledge of the Old Testament Scriptures should have accepted Jesus as the long-awaited Messiah.

1. The leading rabbis of the early first century agreed that the time was ripe for the Messiah to come according to the prophecies of Daniel.

2. Serious inquiry would have revealed to the Jew that Jesus was born in Bethlehem of the line of David, a requirement of the Messiah.

3. Jesus' suffering and death and even his rejection by his own people had been prophesied in detail by Isaiah (ch. 53).

4. More than 400 prophecies and references to the coming of Christ were fulfilled exactly by Jesus of Nazareth.

5. Jesus' apostles were preaching his resurrection even at the cost of their lives. Either they were madmen, or they actually had seen the risen Christ.

6. Even if a first-century Jew had not witnessed any of Jesus' miracles personally, he would have encountered many who had.

7. The apostles (and others upon whom they laid their hands) could perform miraculous signs which surely must have indicated divine endorsement of their message.

After examining the negative and positive factors relating to any first-century Jew's accepting the message of the cross, it is still difficult to understand the "hardening in part" that had befallen Israel

(Romans 11:25). Of course, we must not forget that the earliest Christians were Jews and that the gospel was effective among them during the first few years after Pentecost. Even many of the Jews themselves were responsive to the gospel (like Crispus, Acts 18:8, and Sosthenes, Acts 18:17; 1 Corinthians 1:1—both leaders of the Corinthian synagogue).

Being expelled from the synagogue was being rejected from everything in life that a Jew held dear, not just one phase of life.

Jewish preachers carried the message of Christ throughout the Mediterranean world. But primarily, and especially after the destruction of the temple in A.D. 70, Judaism became virtually a closed door to the Christian faith. Even twenty years before, at the Jerusalem conference (Acts 15), tensions in the Christian Jewish community had almost reached the breaking point. These tensions exemplified the uncertainty many of them felt over the relationship between the Christian faith and adherence to Jewish institutions. This confusion was further demonstrated when Paul met with James and the leading Jewish brethren in Jerusalem (Acts 21:17-26). Already the main current of Christian growth was in the Gentile world, and although New Testament history does not cover it, there would soon be a rupture in the fellowship. Small sects of law-keeping Jewish Christians separated from the main body of the church. They were never very successful in converting very many Jews to their compromise position, and by the fourth century they had died out.

It was certainly not easy for a Jewish person in the first century to give up the long-cherished values he had been taught from childhood. From the practical standpoint, he was likely to be expelled from his synagogue, a punishment the Jewish leaders prescribed for Jews who accepted Jesus as the Messiah (John 9:22, 34). A twentieth-century Gentile Christian might well ask, "What would be so bad about that?" But we must realize, as we have already seen, that the synagogue was not just a place of worship. It was a fellowship, a complete way of life. Being expelled from the synagogue was being rejected from *everything* in life that a Jew held dear, not just one phase of life.

Greek Pride

The Greeks were the victims of their own intellectual pride. They were indeed a remarkable culture. In no period of civilization's history has the human mind soared to such lofty heights as during the classical age of Greece. In such diverse fields as mathematics, philosophy, architecture, and literature they had no peers in the ancient world. Looking down upon the rest of the world from the peaks of their assumed greatness, all other races were dismissed as "barbarians." They were so secure in their excellence that they "colonized" conquered nations by establishing villages of Greeks among them in the assumption that when those primitive peoples saw the superiority of the Greek, or Hellenistic, culture they would naturally adopt it.

Any new truth would come from the Lyceum, the school opened by Aristotle centuries earlier in Athens. The notion that any message of consequence could come from itinerant Jewish fanatics was too ludicrous for any sensible person to entertain. Unfortunately, in their false superior wisdom they had become true fools.

The Foolishness of God

Although Corinth had been founded by colonists from Rome, its culture, like most cultures of the Mediterranean world, had been at least superficially hellenized. Their language, literature, philosophy, and fine arts were all borrowed from the Greeks. They aspired to being a second Athens but lacked the discipline of the classical Greeks. The carnality and grossness of Rome carried over into every aspect of their culture, whether in architecture (which was too ornate to seriously challenge the simple beauty of the Greek masterpieces) or in lifestyle. The word in the Hellenistic world for living an indulgent, sexually promiscuous life is "to Corinthianize."

Not all of the Corinthians were intellectually arrogant; otherwise, there could have been no church established in Corinth.

But the field in which they especially desired to pattern themselves after the "golden Greeks" was philosophy. Corinthians loved to imagine themselves great thinkers, even though Corinth never produced a philosopher of renown. They made judgments in areas where they had no competence. Not only did they take it upon themselves to evaluate Paul's credentials as a preacher (1 Corinthians 4:3-5), but they even passed judgment upon the crucifixion as a suitable plan for humankind's salvation. They regarded the concept of sacrifices being substituted for sin as foolishness and the resurrection of Christ as an impossible absurdity. It goes without saying that not all of the Corinthians were intellectually arrogant; otherwise, there could have been no church established in Corinth. Nevertheless, those who were humble enough to accept the gospel were mainly of the poorer and less prominent classes of society (1:26). Once again, love was the missing ingredient. Their overcoming love had been run out of Corinth on a rail by intellectualism.

Greek Opposition to the Gospel

Those who were prominent in the socio-political and intellectual circles of Corinth were contemptuous of the gospel message. There are several apparent reasons for that attitude:

1. The gospel message was of foreign origin. Palestine was of little significance in the Gentile world. Although Jews were present as artisans and tradesmen in every Gentile city, they were known as quarrelsome religious fanatics and were not generally well liked. In their minds, the execution of an obscure Jew by the Romans was hardly a creditable basis on which to found a world religion.

2. The gospel's public proclaimers were Jews. Those who first preached the gospel in Corinth— Paul, Apollos, Priscilla and Aquila, Timothy—were all Hebrews. Had they been Greek educators from the Lyceum in Athens they might have made a better public impression. Instead, Paul was a foreign tentmaker from the Middle East as were also Aquila and Priscilla. Paul was known best in the city for having been the cause of a Jewish riot during Gallio's term as proconsul. No love could be lost on such a troublemaker.

3. The gospel's adherents were people of no consequence to the upper crust of Corinth. Christianity had no standing among people of quality with the possible exception of Erastus. It appealed only to the lower classes who were always more gullible and superstitious than the better educated citizens.

4. *Christianity was a religion with no visible presence.* The accepted religions of the Corinthian community were based upon imposing temples with an established priesthood. Christianity's places of worship were borrowed rooms in private dwellings. The church's lecture halls were marketplaces and public squares. How could these be appropriate for the God of the Universe?

5. *Christianity was a humiliating religion.* It was formed upon the premise that people were unable to help themselves and must rely entirely upon divine favor. The innate nobility of the human character was discounted, and humankind was portrayed as debased and sensual. In Greek thinking, there was no unbridgeable gap between the human and divine natures. The Greek gods and goddesses were fickle and capricious and as subject to all the moral flaws and inconsistencies as the humans who made them. Admittedly, the Greek philosopher Plato had reasoned that there is a supreme intelligence behind the universe whose perfect laws govern all creation, but the average Corinthian no more understood Plato than the average American understands Einstein. A Greek offered sacrifices to his gods as bribes to inflate their egos so that, at best, they might bless some undertaking of his, or, at the least, to prevent their doing him mischief. Self-pride here, too, defeated love's message of exaltation through humility.

6. *The gospel offered forgiveness of sins.* They were unconcerned with moral behavior, so they saw no need for forgiveness of sins. In fact, the Greek language had no actual word for "sin." The word *hamartia* in the Greek Old and New Testaments derives its meaning of sin from its Jewish-Christian

context. The word in secular use means "to miss the mark." Antisocial behavior might be a violation of society's norms, in bad taste, or even criminal, but the idea inherent in "sin" of creating an unbridgeable gulf between people and their perfect Maker was foreign to Gentile thought. In contrast, the Hebrew Old Testament has at least ten words to convey the concept of sin.

7. *Christianity's validity was based upon the reality of a bodily resurrection.* The Athenians had sneered when Paul preached the resurrection of Christ (Acts 17:32). The Corinthians also found it quite incredible (1 Corinthians 15:12). That does not mean that they did not believe in the survival of the human spirit after the death of the body. Generally, they believed that the "shade" (spirit) of a person would exist in an underworld they called Hades. But the idea of a decomposed body's being reconstituted and raised again to life was preposterous and contrary to all human experience. Their disbelief is well-illustrated in Festus's response to Paul. Although Festus was a Roman, his religious and philosophical upbringing would have differed little from that of the average upperclass Greek. When Paul spoke of Christ's resurrection, Festus exclaimed: "You are out of your mind, Paul! Your great learning is driving you insane" (Acts 26:24).

Corinthian Prospects

For the above reasons it would appear to be an impossible task to establish the church in any city of Greek or Roman orientation. Even after his rebuff in Athens, Paul nevertheless undertook to evangelize Corinth, and the Lord had confirmed that his mission would be successful: ". . . the Lord spoke to Paul in a vision . . . keep on speaking . . . because I have

many people in this city" (Acts 18:10). In fact, the
Lord always has many people potentially in any city.
No city can legitimately be written off as beyond the
reach of the gospel because in every society people
differ from each other. Some are indifferent to any
calling to a higher life. Others are longing for someone to lead them.

It is the role of the Holy Spirit to open the hearts
of the honest seekers to the convicting power of the
gospel. Jesus said, "He will convict the world of guilt
in regard to sin and righteousness and judgment"
(John 16:8). Missionaries to pagan cultures are
struck by the power of the gospel to convict human
hearts in circumstances where acceptance of the
message of salvation would seem virtually impossible. As I, a preacher from the West, enter a village
in Africa, everything about me shouts that I am an
alien: my physical features, my dress, my manner-
isms, and my speech (even though I may have

---

*It is the role of the Holy Spirit to open
the hearts of the honest seekers to the
convicting power of the gospel.*

---

learned the local dialect). I come with the quite
outrageous message that the Creator was born in
human form, died as a sacrifice for our sins, was
buried, and rose to life again from the grave. One
would expect that my hearers would dismiss me as a
raving lunatic. Quite to the contrary, they are
gripped with intense interest as the message of love
unfolds, just as if they are hearing something their
minds have no memory of but which their hearts
have always had a place for. Not everyone will
accept it and respond to its call. But surprisingly few
will deny its truth, even though by any rules of

human logic they should reject it as a preposterous invention of Western legend. Surely this can be attributed only to the ministry of God's Spirit.

There were more earthly reasons, however, why Corinth had many prospective Christians in its cosmopolitan population. A major reason was that the old Greco-Roman pantheon of gods had almost run its course. From the fourth century before Christ, thinking people had begun to question the reality of gods who spent their time in drunken orgies and who from time to time took human partners in adulterous relationships. To intellectuals like Socrates, Plato, and Aristotle, they were simply ancient myths still believed by children and simple folk. Even ordinary people had begun to scoff at their gods as creatures of the imagination, and some were looking elsewhere for more believable divinities.

In Corinth there were a number of temples to Egyptian deities with large followings. Some people joined mystery cults which were beginning to penetrate the Mediterranean world from the Middle East and even from Greece itself. Their secret rites, speaking in unknown tongues, and claims to prophetic knowledge appealed to many who found no comfort in the state religion. But the most fertile field of all for the gospel were Corinthians who were "God fearers"—Gentiles who had had contact with Jews and had become convinced that the Jews' God was really God, but who had not become true converts by submitting to circumcision (like Titius Justus, Acts 18:7).

When Paul refers to the message of the cross as foolishness to the Greek Gentiles, he qualifies the conclusion by adding "to those who are perishing." Those whose intellectual pride prevented their accepting truth from a humble source dismissed the resurrection message as a foolish myth, thereby closing their hearts to saving truth and ensuring that they would perish. In every age there are pretenders to wisdom whose arrogance blinds their eyes to true wisdom and will not allow the seeds of truth to take root in their hearts. They claim to be wise but are in reality fools (Romans 1:22). They reject faith in God, and yet they accept as fact the most unreasonable and quite unprovable "scientific" theories that, even if they could be established, would not explain the existence of a single atom in the universe.

Blinded by Pride

Few of us are Bereans (Acts 17:11), willing to honestly consider any possible new avenue of truth but careful to investigate and evaluate it before embracing it. Neither are Christians immune to spiritual blindness and deafness. It is always more comfortable to follow a well-worn groove of popular beliefs and established rituals than to keep our hearts and minds open to positive change. It is always a prevailing danger for us to become obsessed with the conviction that we have a monopoly on truth and close our hearts to any growth in understanding God's Word. But our religion is far too important to allow it to settle into a comfortable habit. And the consequences are far too serious for us to allow pride or loyalty to tradition to close our hearts to additional truths.

Pride is a blindfold that shuts out the light of truth and blocks the entrance into the kingdom of God. Pride is self-focused and is, perhaps, more nearly the direct opposite of love than even hatred. And pride was the bitter root of opposition to the gospel by both Jews and Gentiles in the first-century Mediterranean world. To the Jew, the gospel did not give proper recognition to his uniqueness as a circumcised son of Abraham. To the Greek, its simple solution to a complex problem was an insult to his superior intelligence. Jews were embarassed by the weak spectacle of Jesus dying a shameful death at the hands of the Romans. The Greeks and Romans found it humiliating to accept that they were so vile that they needed someone else, particularly a Jew, to die for their sins.

> *Pride is a blindfold that shuts out the light of truth and blocks the entrance into the kingdom of God.*

Pride closed the hearts of these people to love of the truth because they found it offensive to accept that they needed a Savior. But are most people in our twentieth-century world so very different? The "Jews" of today's world are smug "Christians" who say, "We know the truth, and we must be right because of who we are." The "Greeks" are those today who, without honest investigation, dismiss God's revelation to us as "fairy tales for children."

Grace to the Humble

The beautiful but simple message of love from the cross was offensive to both Jew and Gentile. For many it was offensive merely because it was so simple. Their vision was so clouded by pride that they did not recognize in it God's message of love for them. "God opposes the proud but gives grace to the humble" (James 4:6). God cannot give what will not be accepted, and only the humble will accept the grace of the cross. We must approach God without any preconditions or hidden agendas before we can experience the boundless grace of the atonement.

"Love is not proud." Before God's love can touch and transform your life and the life of his church, you must set pride aside and run into his open arms of love as the once-prideful but now-wiser prodigal son came to his father. And the Father will welcome you with joy!

Focusing Your Faith

1. In what ways might your beliefs and lifestyle seem foolish to some of your friends and neighbors?

2. If you were to explain the simple saving grace of the cross to a Jewish friend, what would you say?

3. The "Jewish" argument of "But I've *always* done it this way—this is the way I was taught!" is often heard in today's church. What could be said or done to help those with this mindset?

4. Do you consider most people in your church to be Bereans, willing to honestly consider new truths, or Thessalonians, refusing to accept new ideas (Acts 17:11-13)?

5. What has pride blinded you from seeing or doing most recently?

6. What difference should it make in your life to know that God chooses the weak and flawed people of the world to do his work?

7. The Jews believed they were the only "recipients and custodians of all truth." How do you see this attitude being played out in the church today?

1 Corinthians 5:9-13

I have written you in my letter not to associate with sexually immoral people—not at all meaning the people of this world who are immoral, or the greedy and swindlers, or idolaters. In that case you would have to leave this world. But now I am writing you that you must not associate with anyone who calls himself a brother but is sexually immoral or greedy, an idolater or a slanderer, a drunkard or a swindler. With such a man do not even eat.

What business is it of mine to judge those outside the church? Are you not to judge those inside? God will judge those outside. "Expel the wicked man from among you."

Chapter 4

Membership Has
Its Privileges

1 Corinthians 5

Before the coming of European culture to the Western Hemisphere, the Eskimos lived in tightly knit clans. They had no prisons and no death penalty for murderers. Eskimos found guilty of

> The Way:
>
> *Love protects.*
>
> *1 Corinthians 13:7*

willfully taking the life of another were simply excluded from the fellowship of the tribe. They were told that from that day their names would never be mentioned again among the clan. They would not be received into other igloos nor their existence acknowledged in any way. The enormity of this punishment was so dreadful that it robbed their lives of all meaning. Rather than face the bleak prospect of solitary life in the Arctic, the condemned ones would usually take their own lives. Consequently, serious crime was rare among Eskimos.

A few years ago a world-famous Russian literary figure was persecuted and denounced by the Communist regime. Western friends offered to get him out of the country and establish him in comfort in Europe or America. He refused their offer and gave the reason: "Life would have no meaning outside of Mother Russia!"

Sociologists tell us that one of the basic needs of a human being is to belong to a social unit in which he is made to feel valued, appreciated, and protected. When America was a rural society with less mobility, our sense of closeness or belonging was strong because people were interdependent. Everyone in the community pulled together to help when one of them faced trouble. Farmers helped each other plow and harvest their crops. Ranchers helped each other raise new barns and round up cattle. If a neighbor became ill, everyone pitched in to do his work until he was back on his feet again. They protected each other.

Today we are surrounded by distractions that pull us away from relationships and make us more independent. Jobs, hobbies, sports activities, television, and mobility are factors that often get in the way of our togetherness. What first affected our nation is now affecting our churches. Many churches are experiencing the loss of bonding and closeness caused by this movement from interdependence to independence. We no longer protect and care for each other as true love demands.

Unity of Believers

A leading opponent of the early church, while rejecting completely the validity of their religious claims, was nevertheless astonished at the closeness of the disciples' fellowship. He observed that a

Roman is only concerned about taking care of himself, a Jew feels compelled to take care of other Jews, but a Christian will help anyone. He was moved to exclaim in wonder: "Behold, how these Christians love each other!"

When Jesus prayed for the unity of his followers (John 17:20-23), it has often been assumed that he was referring to doctrinal unity. While it is very important that we all embrace the essentials of the Christian faith, Jesus undoubtedly was including much more than that. His petition is in the context of the close love relationship that exists in the Godhead (v. 23).

It is the bond of love that makes Christians a unit that will convince the world that we are truly Christ's disciples (John 13:35). Unless that love permeates the church today, Christian "fellowship" can never mean to us what it meant to the earliest disciples. Their sense of belonging to a mutually supportive Christian fellowship was so strong that it insulated them from the world around them. When they were assaulted by the forces opposing them they turned as a matter of course "to their own people" (Acts 4:23) for re-affirmation and protection.

The church is to be a loving family, a haven of refuge from an uncaring world. When it is less than that, the ties of Christian fellowship are often too weak to withstand the pull of the world. Psalm 68:6 states: "God sets the lonely in families, / he leads forth the prisoners with singing; / but the rebellious live in a sun-scorched land."

Expelling the Wicked

Because of his concern that the Corinthian family was being strongly affected by the pull of the world, Paul warned that the cause of Christ was being undermined by the church's tolerance or acceptance of ungodly behavior among Christians. He advised them to stay away from those who call themselves Christians yet live ungodly lives (1 Corinthians 5:9-13).

From the beginning of his dealings with the Hebrews as a chosen people, God made provision for exclusion of persons whose code of conduct posed a threat to the community's relationship to him. Ridding the community of these compromising elements was termed "cutting off" (Hebrew, *karath*). In the case of certain crimes—perjury in capital cases, rape of a married or engaged woman, sacrifice to idols (and particularly sacrifice of one's children)— "cut off" meant execution. However, many Jewish authorities believe that in the majority of infractions mentioned in one Mosaic code of Exodus and Leviticus, extirpation (the term they use for cutting off) did not require the death penalty but simply expulsion from the congregation of Israel. That person was no longer regarded as an Israelite and was treated as a Gentile. Possibly that's what is meant in Genesis 17:14 where the uncircumcised Hebrew is to be cut off from his people. King Uzziah was "cut off" from the house of the Lord because he was a leper. In other words, he was excluded from the temple (2 Chronicles 26:21).

In synagogue times (dating possibly from the Babylonian exile) disfellowshipping was termed "putting out of the synagogue." This did not mean the actual physical expulsion of a person from a building, but the cancellation of his membership in the community and the forfeiture of all the benefits and protection that membership afforded. It was a penalty that was greatly feared by the ordinary Jews, not because they were so deeply religious, but because of losing all the fringe benefits available to the close knit community. Fellowship provided them with social services they could not afford to lose. The synagogue (and therefore the early church) was much more than an organized religious community. It was a protective support system for every area of life. It was school, hospital, orphanage, social security, and the center of social life. To be cut off from the community (Jewish or Christian) was to be cut adrift from everything that gave life meaning.

It's only in recognizing the marvelous fellowship of Jewish synagogue communities that we can possibly understand the seriousness of disfellowshipping. Like the synagogue, the church was much more than a gathering for worship. They both ministered to the whole person. That's why Jesus cautioned that expulsion from the synagogue (and by logical extension, the church) should only be resorted to as a last, extreme measure (Matthew 18:15-17).

Grounds for Disfellowshipping

From the writings of Paul we can find three principal grounds upon which the New Testament Christians rejected persons from their fellowship.

1. The first was for immorality so grossly flagrant that it was diminishing the church in the esteem of the outside world. The classic example of this is the incestuous relationship between a son and the wife of his father (1 Corinthians 5). Paul points out that even the Graeco-Roman pagans were horrified by such an illicit relationship. The church had to publicly disavow the man for the sake of its reputation in the community.

This example, however, has been used often to deny fellowship to divorced persons whose second marriage is questionable, at least to some. Since the perception of the world in such cases usually is quite different from the situation of Corinthian incest, it is doubtful whether this example justifies a general application, particularly since Corinth was a Roman colony. In Roman society, divorce and remarriage was extremely prevalent (and accepted) and no withdrawals in these cases are recorded in the New Testament.

2. *The second reason for withdrawal was for causing division in the church.* Paul exhorts the Roman Christians (Romans 16:17) to "watch out for" those causing divisions in the body and turn away from them. Presumably the apostle is referring to false doctrines that split the church, but it might very well apply also to legitimate opinions which, pushed to the extreme, could cause a rift in the fellowship. The person himself may be utterly sincere and convinced that he is contending for the truth, but if he is splitting the church by trying to implement an interpretation that is not acceptable to the general congregation, then to preserve unity he needs to be marked and avoided. But note that the issue is *dividing the church*; it is not the issue of holding views dissenting from the majority.

3. *The third reason was for disorderly behavior that was disrupting congregational life.* Paul told the Thessalonians "to keep away from every brother who is idle (literally, "walks out of step") and does not live according to the teaching you received from us" (2 Thessalonians 3:6). If anyone refused this command from Paul, the Thessalonians were to "take special note of him" (literally, "hang a sign on him," that is, "mark him"). They were not to associate with him (*Greek, sunanamingnumi*—"have close fellowship with him") (v. 14).

This third reason is often used today as a catch-all for disfellowshipping any person who opposes the leadership on the pretext that he is "walking disorderly." But the context here applies to persons who refused to work and consistently lived on the generosity of the congregation. Moreover, they were using their idle time to disrupt congregational life by "mischief making."

Disfellowshipping Today

Disfellowshipping a fellow member today generally is not nearly so disciplinary as it was in the first century for the simple reason that our fellowship is not nearly as strong as it was in the first century. The first congregations were modeled after the Jewish synagogue—and the synagogue was a total way of life, a community in every sense of the word. A Jew dreaded above all things being expelled from the synagogue. Jesus warned the apostles that loss of synagogue membership was the price they would have to pay eventually in order to remain faithful to him (Mark 8:34, 35; Luke 14:26, 27).

Paul's order to "not keep company with, or even eat with" the disfellowshipped person would impact strongly on his whole lifestyle. The technical term for "eat with" does not refer to the Lord's Supper or even to eating meals in other relationships than Christian fellowship. In other words, a disfellowshipped Christian might work with other Christians in a secular business where the employees eat their meals in the company lunchroom. It would not be "eating with" him in the sense of close Christian fellowship. Paul likely is referring to the love feasts of the primitive church where eating together was symbolic of oneness, not ordinary family or business-oriented meals. In today's Christian culture, a

"marked" person would not be invited to class parties, congregational dinners, etc. The "don't associate
intimately" would apply to including him or her in
golf tournaments, weekend trips, etc. Inviting a
disfellowshipped person to dinner at your house for
the expressed purpose of addressing the problem of
his or her delinquency, however, is a completely
different matter and would be acting out the love of
God.

Reasons for Disfellowshipping Today

Today there are three principle legitimate reasons for withdrawing Christian fellowship from a
member of the congregation:

1. to protect the image of the church in the
   community so that the church's influence
   and ability to reach the lost is not hin-
   dered. If the world gains the perception
   that the church condones standards of
   morality that even respectable nonreligious
   people would reject, it will not be effective
   in teaching the gospel.

2. to protect the congregation itself from
   becoming contaminated by unacceptable
   norms of behavior. Weaker members might
   assume the sinful behavior is acceptable to
   the leadership.

3. to bring social pressure on the errant
   member to repent so that he can be saved
   and again enjoy the benefits and protection
   of fellowship in the congregation.

It must be pointed out that "disfellowshipping" in
today's church does not generally result in the
dramatic effect it had in the first century. In most

cases those persons will respond negatively by just closing the church out of their lives or else seeking fellowship in another church. There still may be no choice but to disfellowship them if they are disrupting congregational harmony or leading others astray.

In any society that functions effectively, the individual members strive to live up to the expectations of the group rather than face rejection. When the bonds holding a member to this "family" become weaker than his desire to go his own way, the disciplinary tool of disfellowship no longer works. You can't *dis*fellowship someone who isn't *in* fellowship at the time.

You can't disfellowship someone who isn't in fellowship at the time.

Withdrawal of fellowship is, at best, a dismal solution to a problem and should be resorted to only when genuine, love-motivated attempts have been made to restore him to useful and harmonious ministry in the church. It is a big mistake to disfellowship people for "non-attendance." They have, in fact, already disfellowshipped themselves from the congregational body. Any act to document the situation will simply alienate them further and ensure that they won't come back.

Broadly speaking, we have been very selective in choosing grounds for disfellowship. Usually "immorality" in today's church means illicit sex (due perhaps to the mystique surrounding sex in Western Christian society and deriving from our Puritan forefathers). But when Paul uses the expression "immoral person" in 1 Corinthians 5, he is including not only fornicators, but greedy persons, swindlers, idolaters (which includes the materialist, Ephesians 5:5), and slanderers. When we begin withdrawing from stingy givers and gossips as well as from "unscripturally divorced" people, we can at least plead consistency.

Effects of Disfellowshipping

We must answer the question "Do these sinful conditions mentioned in 1 Corinthians 5 and Ephesians 5:5 call for withdrawal of fellowship?" with an emphatic yes. But when we face the next question "What effect will it have?" we must admit that generally it does not have nearly so positive an effect as it had in the early church or in the Jewish synagogue.

The reasons for this ineffectiveness are not hard to find. The reaction of many who are the objects of disfellowship range from "What fellowship?" to "Who needs it? They never cared about me in the first place!"

Many have asked, "How can we make disfellowshipping as effective as it was in New Testament times?" The answer is, "We can't, unless and until we make *fellowship* as effective as it was in New Testament times."

"Love protects" us in the church if that love is God's love. If the loving fellowship is so precious that losing it would totally destroy a person's life, like the Eskimos, then, and only then, can removing that fellowship have the desired impact on a wayward or troublesome Christian. When our true motivation for disfellowshipping is to *protect* our congregation and the errant brother or sister rather than to *punish* the offender, then we are acting out of love. God's love always seeks to *reclaim* and *restore* his children to the fellowship. I wonder: Does ours?

Focusing Your Faith

1. If you were to be disfellowshipped from your church today, what would you miss most?

2. Is immorality a cultural issue and, so, changes from time to time? What forms of immorality are most present in the church today?

3. How can the church be a loving family, a haven of rest for Christians? How would your church need to change?

4. What would you say to a Christian friend who is unwilling to turn from a particular sin?

5. At what point would you stop associating with a person who continued to do wrong?

6. Since you can't really disfellowship those who are not attending anyway, what can you do to encourage them? What part should prayer play?

7. If we are to disassociate ourselves from immoral people in the church, what are we to do about those outside the church?

1 Corinthians 6:1-8

If any of you has a dispute with another, dare he take it before the ungodly for judgment instead of before the saints? Do you not know that the saints will judge the world? And if you are to judge the world, are you not competent to judge trivial cases? Do you not know that we will judge angels? How much more the things of this life! Therefore, if you have disputes about such matters, appoint as judges even men of little account in the church! I say this to shame you. Is it possible that there is nobody among you wise enough to judge a dispute between believers? But instead, one brother goes to law against another—and this in front of unbelievers!

The very fact that you have lawsuits among you means you have been completely defeated already. Why not rather be wronged? Why not rather be cheated? Instead, you yourselves cheat and do wrong, and you do this to your brothers.

Chapter 5

Suits That

Don't Suit

1 Corinthians 6:1-11

While I was living in Port Elizabeth, South Africa, Don Gardner called from East London and asked me to go to Durban with him to research the feasibility of establishing a congregation there. He pro-

> ## The Way:
>
> *Love does not keep record of wrongs.*
>
> *1 Corinthians 13:5*

posed picking me up, as he had to come to Port Elizabeth anyhow, and after spending a few days in Durban, we would pay a visit to the missionary families in Johannesburg and Pretoria. I was pleased at the opportunity to accompany him and had my bag packed and ready to go when he arrived. I overlooked only one important detail—I didn't put my suitcase in his car.

Somewhere in Zululand, before we reached Durban, I became sharply aware that I had left my clothing behind. It was much too far to return for it. I was clad in an old pair of gardening pants and a well-worn T-shirt. I couldn't even get into a hotel dining room in that rig. There was nothing to do but to buy a suit. But where? We were driving through endless fields of sugar cane with a settlement here and there. When we reached a small village with a few stores, we stoppped and inquired whether there was a clothing store. We were directed to a small Indian shop where the owner greeted us with effusive enthusiasm. Did he have a suit for me? But of course he had. He had one suit. It was a green gabardine. It had been made for the giant wrestler Man Mountain Dean.

"But I can never wear that!" I protested. "Ah, but I can alter it to fit you—one time!" he assured me blandly. "You'll see." After thirty minutes, I saw. The length of the trousers was right; the length of the sleeves was right. The hemline of the coat and the crotch of the trousers were perfectly aligned—they both reached my knees. The hip pockets were brought together to make one rather unusual divided pocket. But it was a suit, and as he kept reminding me, what choice did I have? I had none. I bought it.

If I presented a rather bizarre and chaplinesque appearance in the hotel and restaurants we visited, the clerks and waiters were able to suppress their merriment until I was out of earshot. Not so my friends. Martelle Petty, Guy Caskey, and their wives had booked dinner at a restaurant in Pretoria and theater tickets for the evening. Martelle Petty took one look at my recently acquired finery and went into fits of unseemly laughter. Then all of our so-called friends simply wept with mirth. I bore with the uncomfortable exhibition until they had exhausted themselves, after which we went to dinner. Still, at intervals, a snort or snicker from one of them was enough to send the whole pack into gales of raucous hilarity.

I was able to walk on the level reasonably well, provided I took short, rather mincing, steps. Climbing stairs was virtually impossible; I could only do it by turning sideways and carefully lifting one foot at a time to the next elevation. The theater, naturally, had a soaring flight of steps leading up to the lobby. I could not skip up them with the easy abandon of the rest of our party, so by the time I had reached the crowded lobby they were nowhere in sight. Then I heard Martelle Petty shout, "There he is!" And presently we were reunited. The others told me that Martelle had located me by dropping to his knees and looking through the legs of the crowd. When he saw a crotch almost dragging the ground they knew they had found their man. I was really developing a strong aversion, even bordering on hatred, for that green gabardine suit. "Vanity of vanities, all is vanity, saith the Preacher."[1]

The jury's still out on whether wearing that suit was worth it or not. Besides being rather embarrassing to me and my friends, I wonder what it did to my credibility as a minister of God. Had I tried to talk about Jesus to anyone while wearing that suit, I'm sure the person would have thought I was a lunatic. Just as that suit was illfitting attire for me, Christians being involved in lawsuits with other Christians is another misfit. People are always scrutinizing Christians to see if their actions fit their words. When outsiders see Christians going after other Christians in court battles, they see the hypocrisy in the lifestyles of those who are professing Christian love.

When a society is characterized by constant litigation, or legal disputes, it indicates a breakdown in moral fiber and a lack of honor and trust. Jesus warned his followers (Matthew 5:25, 26) to settle their disputes among themselves rather than to resort to the folly of court suits. It has been a long time since it could be generally and truthfully said that "a man's word is his bond" or that "an agreement could be sealed with a handshake." The following is a true story from a nineteenth-century small town in the American Southwest:

A farmer had just completed a new barn and wanted to insure it, so he went to the local insurance broker, a man widely respected for his honesty, and asked him to issue the policy. The insurance man shook the farmer's hand and said, "All right. You are covered. I'll have the papers ready for you to sign tomorrow." That night the barn burned. The following day the farmer met the broker in the street and said to him, "I'll bet you're glad I hadn't signed those papers." The broker's face flushed, and he drew himself up stiffly. "Sir," he declared, "you are insured! We shook on it!"

Unlike the farmer and the insurance broker, there was a lack of trust and concern for each other in the Corinthian church. Their actions showed how immature they were in the Christian faith. Corinth was a litigious society where people kept a careful record of wrongs done to them, and the church there was no different in that respect than the pagans. In 1 Corinthians 6 Paul attempts to persuade them of a more excellent way.

City on a Hill

A part of the church's approach to the world is high visibility. As Paul wrote to the Thessalonians, we tell about Christ so our faith in God may become known everywhere. Jesus pointed out that his followers are comparable to a city on a hill or a lamp on a lampstand, visible to everybody. Ideally, others observe our good behavior and want to come to God themselves (Matthew 5:14-16). We cannot escape the sobering realization that what people see in individual members of the church will form the basis of their evaluation of the entire fellowship of believers.

The power of our influence can't be over-emphasized. Israel's failure to live up to their covenant with the Lord caused his name to be profaned among the heathen (Ezekiel 36:20). In contrast, the goodness Ruth saw in her Hebrew mother-in-law Naomi prompted Ruth the Moabitess to exclaim to her: "Your people will be my people and your God my God." (Ruth 1:16). And the testimony of a little Hebrew slave girl led the Syrian general Naaman to the salvation of both his body and his soul (2 Kings 5:1-14). All these examples bear out that our influence is a heavy power that can change lives, for the better or for the worse.

When bickering and back-biting disrupt the harmony of the fellowship, love is not in that place. When members keep a checklist of grievances against each other, and, like the Scotch dame of Burns's poem, "nurse their wrath to keep it warm," the love God wants us to show is absent. When the new minister for a congregation is met by a barrage of gripes and accusations from the members against one another, he knows he is going to have to preach some powerful sermons on "Love does not keep record of wrongs" or his ministry will not be successful. Paul faced just such a challenge at Corinth.

Corinth was a Roman city with an overlay of Greek culture. The Corinthians spoke the Greek language and studied Greek philosophy, but their lifestyle was corrupted by Roman, North African, and Middle Eastern influences. The city with its twin ports Cenchrea and Lecheum, located on both sides of the narrow isthmus, controlled commercial traffic between east and west. The resulting prosperity had attracted fortune-seekers from the whole Mediterranean world. What Tyre had been in an earlier age, Corinth had become in the first century A.D. It was a fleshpot of moral depravity.

In such a corrupt setting, it was essential that the fledgling Christian church exemplify a code of behavior that contrasted sharply with the immorality of the world around them. In a dog-eat-dog world of selfishness and greed, it was important for the community of disciples to reflect values that were based upon spiritual realities if they were to have any impact upon society. In particular, they would be judged by their treatment of and their care for each other. To successfully present a God of love to a loveless world, they would first have to exhibit that love for each other.

To successfully present a God of love to a loveless world, they would first have to exhibit that love for each other.

We do not want to indict those whom we love. Rather we seek to put the best construction possible upon their behavior, so that we become their defenders instead of their accusers. We try to excuse their faults and help to correct them by gentle persuasions. Love is one weapon against which Satan cannot devise a successful defense. Jesus said, "All men will know that you are my disciples, if you love one another" (John 13:35). Nothing communicates like genuine love.

Lack of Love

One strong evidence of the lack of love that existed in the Corinthian church was their readiness to sue one another in the secular courts. This was especially distressing to the apostle Paul because not only did it reveal a lack of concern for the unity of the body, it tarnished the reputation of the church in the eyes of the world. Paul rebuked them in strong words (1 Corinthians 6:1-8).

There is a wide gap between what Paul expected of the Corinthian church in their dealings with one another and what they were in fact practicing. This may be attributed in large part to two principal factors: a lack of cohesion in the membership of the congregation and a completely different perspective.

Church unity was not easily achieved in the Corinthian situation. They were a diverse group made up of many elements. The names that are recorded in Acts 18:8, 17 bear out racial differences. Achaichus, Crispus, Fortunatue, Justus, Gaius, and Quintus are Roman; Sosthenes, Phoebe, and Erastus are Greek names. Crispus and Sosthenes were of the Jewish race as would have been many others since the work in Corinth began in the synagogue (Acts 18:4). The eloquent Apollos was an Alexandrian Jew and would likely have attracted some of the large Egyptian population living in Corinth.

The potential for division that was already naturally present became a reality (1 Corinthians 1:10-15). But division was no doubt a symptom rather than a basic cause. They didn't even eat the Lord's Supper together as a congregation. The strength of group loyalty and mutual affection had so characterized that first church in Jerusalem (Acts 2) that their heathen critics exclaimed, "Behold how they love one another!" However, these qualities were not present to any considerable degree in the Corinthian assembly. Given the dissension and mutual distrust in the congregation, it is not surprising that they were unwilling to entrust the legal settlement of their affairs to other Christians. Perhaps they felt they would get a more impartial hearing in a Roman magistrate's court.

Paul's Jewish background had given him an entirely different perspective from a Corinthian Gentile. Paul was influenced by the many centuries of the Hebrew legal system. Jesus himself had outlined in Matthew 18:15-17 the correct legal procedure open to the Jew (in the context, "church," or assembly, refers to the synagogue). So there is every reason for extending these principles to the church.

The Jewish Example

Originally, among the Semitic (Jewish) clans, the patriarch of each unit acted as a judge in sorting out the problems of his subjects. This had worked very well as long as they formed close-knit but widely-scattered extended families of cattle grazers. However, it broke down quickly when they were massed into one horde of hundreds of thousands at the beginning of the wilderness wanderings. Moses, as their leader, naturally took the role of judge, but it became quickly apparent that this wasn't going to work anymore. He sat hearing cases all day long with throngs of people standing around waiting for their petitions to be heard. They still had the elders of their various divisions (Exodus 18:12). The text does not explain why they didn't serve as judges, but they clearly did not. It took a visit from Moses' father-in-law, Jethro, to bring order out of chaos. Jethro suggested setting up various levels of judges with authority over groups ranging from ten people to one thousand. Only the most serious cases were to be heard by Moses himself, and so that is what Moses did.

In pre-New Testament times, Herod the Great (and his father Antipater) had obtained a number of concessions for the Jews from both Julius Caesar and Augustus Caesar. One of them was the right to judge their own affairs in noncapital cases. The first level of judgment was the synagogue where the leaders settled problems among their members. The highest Jewish court was the Sanhedrin. After the destruction of the temple, the Sanhedrin was no longer functional, but the synagogue continued to function as a court wherever Jews formed communities throughout the world. In foreign cities they generally formed autonomous communities, sometimes because they were consigned to "ghettoes" and sometimes by their own choice. In large cities where there were several synagogues, rabbinical courts of community leaders were set up to decide major issues. These courts still function today. Even a Gentile with a complaint against a practicing Jew can have his case heard in the rabbinical court. The Gentile must first sign an agreeemnt to abide by the decision of the court.

Even when Jews have not been able to maintain their own courts legally, they have done so secretly for two basic reasons. One is that the nature of many of their internal problems are beyond the competence of a Gentile court. The other is that they have sought to keep their in-house squabbles from attracting unfavorable outside attention. Paul had been accustomed throughout his life as a Jew to seeing his people settle their own problems and not parade them publicly before a hostile world. It pained him deeply that the Corinthian Christians had no qualms about suing each other in a Roman court and apparently were oblivious to the scorn and derision to which it exposed the faith.

The Gentile Example

The perspective of the Gentile members of the Corinthian church would have been quite different from Paul's. Their multiplex culture derived from two principal strands—Greek and Roman. The Greeks were accustomed to settling minor community problems in public assembly (the *ecclesia*, usually translated "church" in the New Testament but originally applied to a public meeting of voting citizens). The Romans, on the other hand, disliked public assemblies because of their potential for producing riots and violence. Their solution was if any "have a grievance against anybody, the courts are open and there are proconsuls" (Acts 19:38).

The Corinthians apparently followed both the Greek and the Roman options. Even the Corinthian Jews, contrary to the general practice of their people, were infected with the tendency to bring synagogue matters before the Roman courts (Acts 18:12, 13), so it is perhaps not so strange that the poorly-assimilated elements of the congregation of the church would become involved in court fights.

Secular courts are necessary to judge human behavior and to prevent anarchy. However, they are subject to all the weaknesses of the human beings who administer the court system. Judges, like everybody else, are subject to bias. Juries often react to emotional pressure instead of giving impartial decisions. The classic saying that justice is blind is all too often true.

Demosthenes was not only the greatest orator of the Golden Age of Greece, he was also the best criminal lawyer in Athens. He was once defending a man on a capital case when he noticed that he had lost his audience. It was hot in the court, and those supposed to be listening to the case were staring out the windows, yawning, or even nodding off occasionally. Demosthenes stopped his argument and began to tell this story: "A traveler once rented a donkey to ride from Athens to Megara. With the owner leading the animal they traveled on until noon of a very hot day, at which time the man dismounted from the donkey, unpacked his lunch and sat down in the donkey's shade to eat it. "That will be another drachma," the owner informed him. "For what?" the traveler exclaimed. "For the donkey's shade," the owner replied. "You rented the donkey, not his shade. That's extra." The man was infuriated and shouted, "Whoever heard of paying for a donkey's shade?" "You've heard it now!" "Well, I won't pay!" "Then I'll see you in court." By then Demosthenes had his audience spellbound. Thereupon he resumed presenting his defense of his client. The judges stopped him. "The donkey's shade—" they explained. "Everyone wants to know how the matter ended."

Demosthenes spoke to them very sternly: "I cannot believe this court. A man is on trial for his life, and all you are interested in is a silly story about a donkey's shadow!"

Options for Settling Claims

Obviously, the Roman courts had faults and inconsistencies, as do today's courts. To expose church matters before unbelievers defeated the impact of preaching love and weakened the power of the gospel message. Paul's preference was that the Corinthian church submit to chosen leaders who were mature and experienced (1 Corinthians 16:15-18) and who would be "wise enough" (6:5) to settle grievances between brethren.[2]

Under the existing situation there was no vehicle for handling such matters except the corporate assembly, which would simply mean that majority decisions would be made by "men of little account in the church" (that is, recent converts and spiritually immature persons). The New International Version (NIV) rendition of 6:4 is probably incorrect in making it a sarcastic statement. "Therefore, if you have disputes about such matters, appoint as judges even men of little account in the church!" The New American Standard translation makes it a question: "If then you have law courts dealing with matters of this life, do you appoint them as judges who are of no account in the church?" which is probably the original meaning. They had, in effect, done just that by leaving matters to a general vote of the congregation, or, even worse, taking them to the magistrate's court.

Paul's second option for settling claims against fellow members of the church is to drop them altogether. "Why not rather be wronged? Why not rather be cheated?" (1 Corinthians 6:7b) The apostle's concern was for the public image of the church as well as for the un-Christian squabbling of the members. The advice he gave might be accepted by a very mature Christian, but it was unlikely to get a hearty response in Corinth. Such advice will work only where individuals value the interests of the congregation as a whole above their personal interests and pride.

We live in an age when lawsuits are becoming

more and more commonplace. Matters that were once settled on an interpersonal basis now find their way into the courts. It is extremely unfortunate when such lawsuits are between Christians, not only because it is a symptom of the breakdown of Christian principles, but because it plays into the hands of those who wish to damage the standing and reputation of the church in the community.

A complication that our first-century brothers and sisters did not have to contend with is the ever-present news media, which tends to embroider and expand the facts to make a good story. The result is often irreparable damage to the image of the church. That would not be necessary if we took Paul's first advice to settle our disputes within our church family. It is only fair to point out that many are so concerned about the church's reputation that they take the apostle Paul's advice and suffer wrong and, consequently, are cheated.

Following Suit

There seems to be no good reason for not following the example of the synagogue practice of submitting problems to our own church leaders for solutions. After all, we expect elders to be the shepherds of our most precious and enduring possessions—our souls. Surely if we submit to their guidance in spiritual matters, it would be a natural course of action to depend on their advice in lesser things that affect relationships between Christians. At least elders could be expected to be more sensitive to spiritual and moral elements in the situation than would secular judges, who do not have the leeway to make a decision based on right and wrong, but rather only on its legal merits.

Whether the church could go as far in establishing

courts as Judaism has done in cities where there are
several congregations might be arguable. The Jews
form a rabbinical court made up of competent rabbis
who may belong to different synagogues. This practice could have application today. Even with the
example of congregational autonomy in mind, consider these points:

1. Such a panel would have no jurisdiction over
any congregation.

2. The panel would have no authority beyond that
which the opposing parties allowed them by signing
agreements to abide by their decision.

3. It would provide a larger pool of capable Christians, some of whom might have legal training.

4. Their decisions might be less vulnerable to
charges of favoritism than might be the case within
a congregation.

5. It would avoid questions of jurisdiction in cases
where the adversaries are members of different
congregations.

A relevant question must be asked: Are there
cases where Christians may meet each other in
secular courts? The answer must obviously be yes.
There are situations involving the establishment of
jurisdiction over children, validity of titles, and
numerous other circumstances that require a legal
settlement or determination. Oftentimes it is with
the concurrence of both parties that such cases are
filed. There are other situations that might legitimately be settled within the church itself but where
one of the parties will not agree to such arbitration.
Jesus advised that such a person be dealt with as
one would deal with any person of the world (Matthew 18:17). Sometimes such matters are much
more than cases of violated personal dignity or hurt

feelings, and the injured person has no choice but to seek legal redress.

There are certain broad principles that may be derived from Paul's teaching concerning lawsuits between Christians. The first is that we should place the overall interests of Christ's church above narrow personal interests. Sometimes this may mean giving up our personal "rights." The second is that, wherever possible, personal grievances among Christians should be settled by the church itself. Both options are mature decisions that will only be made by mature Christians who love Christ and his church above our own petty interests.

"Love does not keep record of wrongs." When we stop keeping lists of grievances against each other and learn to love one another completely, we can eliminate the problems of settling disputes altogether. Then when people see us they will say, "Behold, how these people love each other!"

Notes:

[1] Excerpt from *Wings of the Morning: The Saga of an African Pilgrim* by Eldred Echols (Fort Worth: Wings Press, 1989).

[2] The Corinthians did, in fact, heed Paul's advice eventually and elect elders. This is not recorded in the New Testament, but it is stated in a letter from Clement of Rome to the Corinthian church in A.D. 95.

Focusing Your Faith

1. If love always trusts, should Christians formalize their agreements with signed contracts? Why?

2. Have you ever allowed yourself to be "wronged" rather than to demand your rights? How did you feel then? How do you feel now?

3. What is the most difficult emotion to overcome when you feel you have been wronged by a close friend or family member?

4. If you were to choose five people from your congregation to serve as a "rabbinical court" panel, who would they be? Why?

5. If Christians knew that their lawsuits would be heard by their church leaders, how do you think it would affect the annual number of lawsuits filed by Christians? Why?

6. Would you ever consider allowing Christian peers to arbitrate a disagreement between you and another Christian? Why or why not?

7. Examine your own "checklist of grievances" against the difficult person in your life. Write them down on paper, then pray that God will help you forgive them.

1 Corinthians 7:1-4, 8-11

Now for the matters you wrote about: It is good for a man not to marry. But since there is so much immorality, each man should have his own wife, and each woman her own husband. The husband should fulfill his marital duty to his wife, and likewise the wife to her husband. The wife's body does not belong to her alone but also to her husband. In the same way, the husband's body does not belong to him alone but also to his wife.

Now to the unmarried and the widows I say: It is good for them to stay unmarried, as I am. But if they cannot control themselves, they should marry, for it is better than to burn with passion.

To the married I give this command (not I, but the Lord): A wife must not separate from her husband. But if she does, she must remain unmarried or else be reconciled to her husband. And a husband must not divorce his wife.

Chapter 6

The Divorce
Dilemma

1 Corinthians 7

On the bank of the Jumna River outside the city of Agra in India stands a magnificent mausoleum in white marble, the Taj Mahal. It has been said that it "is within more measurable distance of perfection than any other work of man." It was built by Shah Jahan in the seventeenth century as the memorial tomb for his beloved wife, Mumtaz, but to the millions who have viewed it, it symbolizes the beauty of a completely devoted marital love.

The wisdom literature of the Old Testament takes for granted that marriage is monogamous, although one of the most beautiful marriages in history was polygamous, that of Jacob and Rachel. Jacob erected a splendid tomb for his beloved wife,

> **The Way:**
>
> *Love is not self-seeking.*
>
> *1 Corinthians 13:5*

Rachel, outside Bethlehem which stood for centuries. The site is still marked today by a memorial built in the Middle Ages. Marriage between a man and woman was instituted by God, we are told, because "it is not good for the man to be alone" (Genesis 2:18). Since marriage is the happiest and best condition for most people, Christian teachers and leaders should be very sure of their scriptural grounds before declaring any person unfit for marriage. "Forbidding to marry" for the wrong reasons is one of the marks of the apostate church (1 Timothy 4:1–3).

Building Block of a Healthy Society

Marriage is the basic building block of an organized society. When the institution of marriage breaks down in a culture, society itself inevitably disintegrates. The collapse of the Roman Empire cannot be attributed to a single cause, to be sure. But a major contributing factor to its destruction was a declining respect for the sanctity of marriage and the increasing frequency of divorce. Stability of the country rests primarily upon the stability of marriages within the country, for a tightly-knit family does more to influence conduct than any legal code the nation can legislate. The rising percentage of marriages that end in divorce in the Western world is an ominous omen for the direction in which we are headed. A high divorce rate is both a symptom and a cause of the increasing selfishness and lawlessness that plague our civilization.

In order to devise strategies to prevent diseases and so protect the health of society, we must first identify their causes. But knowing what caused a disease does not address the need for healing of the afflicted person. Divorce is rampant both inside and outside the church. Many Christians who never intended or expected to be a partner in a failed marriage have, nevertheless, found themselves divorced. The church has all too often perceived its role to be that of inquisitor and judge, determining and assigning guilt, rather than that of the physician, restoring and healing the sick. The easy course is to isolate, to relegate the "lepers" to the outer wasteland. Unfortunately, that is where they are most likely to wander until death overtakes them. Probably their best hope of recovering from their wounds is the involved and loving ministry of concerned fellow-Christians.

Paul advises that "since there is so much immorality, each man should have his own wife, and each woman her own husband" (1 Corinthians 7:2). It is worth pointing out that Paul is not addressing the issue of the right of a divorced person to marry. Rather, he is answering the Corinthians' question of whether, in view of his having advised the celibate not to marry, it is permissible to marry at all. The apostle points out in his discussion that he had not meant to teach that getting married was an unworthy choice. In view of the perilous times, he advised those who felt no pressure to marry, not to marry.

**Marriage is for self-givers, not for self-seekers.**

Although generally, any unmarried person is free to marry, it is not always the best choice. Marriage is for self-givers, not for self-seekers. Where one or both partners enter the relationship expecting to receive more from it than he or she is willing to contribute, then the marriage is not being built upon a foundation that will stand the stress and strain of life's challenges. When a man or woman marries simply to find happiness but with no concern for the happiness of the other, then it is certain to bring misery for both.

Marriage for Life

Apparently, some of the Corinthians had concluded, in view of previous letters between them and Paul, that it might be permissible to withdraw from a marriage. Paul quickly corrects this notion: "To the married I give this command (not I, but the Lord): A wife must not separate from her husband. But if she does, she must remain unmarried or else be reconciled to her husband. And a husband must not divorce his wife" (1 Corinthians 7: 10, 11).

God intends for marriage to be for life. No one has the right to simply renounce their marriage. Paul acknowledges that unusual circumstances might arise which would render a separation inevitable, although it is a general rule that marriage partners should stay together. He does not indicate what such circumstances might be. We can only speculate that such situations might include criminal behavior, drunken or other abuse of the spouse and/or children, political danger, etc. Whatever the reason for a separation, it is not mandatory to dissolve the marriage through divorce. Circumstances may require a permanent separation, but they may also change and allow a reconciliation.

Mixed Marriages

A common problem in the early church was that of mixed marriages—a Christian married to an unbeliever, a pagan. Paul's solution for preventing the problems' arising was simple: don't marry an unbeliever (2 Corinthians 6:14). That did not address the heart of the quandary, however. Some marriages occurred while the partners were still pagans, but subsequently one partner, but not both, had become a Christian.

In a society dominated by emperor worship, it was politically expedient to belong to the state religion. That was particularly true if the pagan husband was employed in any branch of government service where he had to attend official ceremonies with his wife. It was common for the pagan partner to demand that his spouse renounce Christianity or risk a break up of the marriage.

Some of the Corinthian Christians wondered whether such a mixed marriage was really a valid marriage at all. Paul assures them that such a marriage is indeed valid. The unbelieving husband is "sanctified" through the Christian wife and the pagan wife through her Christian husband. Other-wise, their children would be illegitimate, which is not the case. This is an _argumentum ad hominem_, that is, an argument based upon perception.

The Corinthians were worried that such a mixed marriage was "un-Christian" and that, therefore, God would not bless it. Paul is saying that the special providence of God for his children extends to his care in regard to their marriage, and it still applies to a mixed marriage for the sake of the Christian involved. God recognizes the legitimacy of the marriage, and so there is no question of the legitimacy of the children of that marriage.

The Christian was not to be the aggressor in breaking up his or her marriage with a heathen. If, however, the pagan threw down the gauntlet by declaring, "You leave the church, or I'll leave you!" then the Christian was under no obligation to sacri-fice his or her principles for the sake of holding the marriage intact. "Let him go," the apostle instructs. "The Christian is not a slave in such a situation"

(1 Corinthians 7:15). A slave had to follow his master wherever he went, but a Christian married to an unbeliever was not the unbeliever's slave. Some have argued from the usual translation "the brother or sister is not bound in such cases" that the Christian is now divorced through no fault of his own and is, therefore, free to remarry. That conclusion may be correct, but it is not a necessary inference from Paul's statement, since he actually uses the word *douloo* (to be enslaved) rather than the word *deomai* (to be bound or tied) which he used in verse 27 to describe the marriage bond.

Obviously, some Corinthian Christians were making the argument (as many still do) that it is wise to leave the church temporarily for the sake of the unbelieving mate. The hope is that time will mellow him or her, and eventually a suitable occasion may arise for converting the partner. Paul counters this alluring logic by asking, "How do you know, wife, whether you will save your husband? Or, how do you know, husband, whether you will save your wife" (v. 16)? In fact, the most likely way to convert an unbelieving mate is for the Christian to remain firm and committed to the Lord.

Paul's advice to the unmarried was based on the troubling times under which the church struggled (and circumstances were soon to become much worse). He wrote: "Now about virgins [the noun includes both single men and single women]. . . . Because of the present crisis, I think that it is good for you to remain as you are" (vv. 25, 26).

A whole system of theology has been built upon the assumption that Paul was praising the celibate life as somehow more spiritually excellent than the marital state. This has resulted in the development of "orders" of nuns and monks who take chastity vows and devote themselves to the "spiritual" life. Some go to the extreme of shutting themselves off from the rest of humanity in a cloistered life (which prevents their being of much practical use in ministry). Others take vows of silence, which keeps them from communicating their message to others. In fairness, many of them do devote their time to teaching and ministering to the sick and lead self-sacrificing lives for their beliefs.

Paul indeed stated that "one who is unmarried is concerned about the things of the Lord . . . but one who is married is concerned about the things of the world, how he may please his wife, and his interests are divided" (vv. 32-34, NASB). But it would be wrong to conclude that he is saying that the single state is spiritually superior to the married state. The first-century church was an intensely missionary institution under trying and dangerous conditions. A single person had much more flexibility in moving from place to place than a married man or woman. A person with a family could not change residence quickly or easily. A married person had the burden of earning a living for dependents. He or she could not as single-mindedly risk death or imprisonment as someone who had no family responsibilities. There are still situations in the world where a single person can serve more effectively than a married person, but they are in the extreme minority of cases.

Drawing Conclusions About Marriage

Paul makes some important points in this section (vv. 17-40).

1. It isn't important what your circumstance is when the Lord calls you to his service (married or

unmarried, circumcised or uncircumcised, slave or free). What is important is doing what God has commanded, without trying to change your situation. (Paul had made one exception to this rule in verse 9: If you are single and tempted to immorality, you should marry).

2. A marriage between a Christian and an unbeliever is a valid marriage, but if the unbeliever wants to desert the marriage, let him go.

3. In view of the critical times being experienced at Corinth and which were shortly to become much worse, the apostle advised:

- If you are unmarried you will find your life far less complicated in the prevailing circumstances if you remain single.

- If you are married, stay married.

- If you are unmarried and want to marry, then do so. It's no sin.

- If you are engaged to a girl and feel under obligation to marry her, do so.

- If you are engaged, but feel that circumstances do not justify getting married, then it's no sin to call it off.

- A widow would be well-advised to remain single, but if she wants to marry a Christian man, she is perfectly free to do so.

Divorce and Remarriage

Paul admonishes that "since there is so much immorality, each man should have his own wife, and each woman her own husband" (7:2). This has generally been interpreted in mainline churches with the qualification "assuming that they are free to marry." Usually it has been held that it applies only to persons who have never married, those who have been widowed, and to "the innocent party" in a divorce. This exclusion of one partner in a dissolved marriage is based upon the traditional interpretation of the passage, "Anyone who divorces his wife and marries another woman commits adultery, and the man who marries a divorced woman commits adultery (Luke 16:18; see also Matthew 5:31, 32; 19:3-9; Mark 10:2-12).

Those who hold this position assume that Jesus is making a sharp contrast between what Moses allowed concerning divorce as a concession to a hard-hearted people and what Jesus himself is now setting forth as God's eternal law (see Deuteronomy 24:1-4). That view can be summarized into the following points:

- Adultery is the single allowable cause for the dissolution of a marriage.

- The innocent party is free to remarry.

- The guilty party must remain unmarried for the rest of his or her life.

- If the guilty party ever remarries, both he (or she) and the other partner in the disallowed marriage are living in adultery and will continue to live in adultery as long as the illicit union is maintained.

A _casual_ reading of the Matthew, Mark, and Luke passages cited may indicate that the position stated is true. Nevertheless, _honest_ interpretation requires us to compare what these scriptures out of context appear to teach and what they are actually saying in the context in which they were given.

Jesus did not initiate the dialogue between himself and the Pharisees. Matthew 19:3 begins the discourse with, "Some Pharisees came to him to test him. They asked, 'Is it lawful for a man to divorce his wife for any and every reason?' " What were the Pharisees asking? Were they asking whether Jesus intends to teach Moses' law of marriage in the coming kingdom age? They did not regard Jesus as having in any way authority equal to that of Moses. They regarded the Torah (the Law) as completely and definitely authoritative. They simply regarded Jesus as a popular and controversial rabbi who was independent of the established rabbinical schools of theology. The fact that they asked the question at all is significant. Why would they ask it since they regarded Moses as completely authoritative and his law as binding? The obvious conclusion is that there was an area of controversy in Judaism over what Moses' law actually taught. If this be true, then the Jewish writings should give some evidence of this dissension, and in fact they do. In the treatise *Gittin* (9:10) of the Babylonian Talmud it states: "The school of Shammai says: A man cannot divorce his wife unless he has found unchastity in her, for it is written, because he hath found in her indecency in anything (Deuteronomy 24:1). And the school of Hillel says: He may divorce her even if she spoiled a dish for him, for it is written, because he hath found indecency in her in anything."

The great teachers of Israel at the beginning of the Christian era were the *Zugot*, or Pairs. The greatest of these Pairs were Shammai and Hillel, who presided over the Sanhedrin and who dominated Jewish theology in the time of Christ through the two great rabbinical schools which they founded.

Shammai was generally very conservative in his interpretation of the Law. Hillel was a great scholar from Babylonia who ruled the Sanhedrin for forty years (until A.D. 10). He is known as the father of biblical hermeneutics and was much more liberal in his interpretation of the law than Shammai.

Pharisees Did Not Ask

It is important to establish what the Pharisees were asking and what they were not asking. They were *not* asking:

- What laws of divorce was Jesus planning to impose in his coming kingdom? They did not regard him in any sense as a lawgiver.

- Is the woman "put away" allowed to re-marry? The very purpose of the law set forth in Deuteronomy 24:1-4 was to protect the women from being kept by a husband who had replaced her with another woman as his wife but kept his former wife in virtual bondage. A better translation of the Hebrew is: "If it happens that she becomes displeasing because he finds indecency in her, then let him write her a certificate of divorce and put it in her hand and send her out of his house, so that she may go and become another man's wife." Another reason for the certificate of divorce was to make the separation irrevocable once she had married another man. "Her first husband who divorced her is not allowed to marry her again. . . . That would be detestable in the eyes of the Lord" (Deuteronomy 24:4).

Pharisees Did Ask

The Pharisees *were* asking: What did Moses mean by using the word *indecency* (Hebrew, *ervah*) in Deuteronomy 24:1? Did he mean "sexual immorality" (as Shammai said) or did he mean "any unpleasant thing" (as Hillel said)?

Jesus prefaced his answer by reminding them that from the beginning God had intended marriage to be for life. Paul restates this in 1 Corinthians 7:39: "A woman is bound to her husband as long as he lives." Jesus went on to say that Moses allowed divorce as a concession to hard-heartedness in people. He then stated: "Whoever divorces his wife except for sexual immorality and marries another, commits adultery" (Matthew 19:9). Matthew 5:32 adds "He caused her to commit adultery," and Luke 16:18 adds "He who marries one who is divorced from a husband commits adultery."

The words for "sexual immorality" (*porneia*) and "adultery" (*moichia*) are very different in their meaning. *Porneia* means basically "prostitution" (from the Greek word *porne*—a prostitute) and indicates a sexually immoral lifestyle. *Moichia* (adultery) is the sexual violation of the rights of a married person by the spouse and the person with whom the spouse commits the offense. Adultery can only be committed against a marriage. Adultery is not possible against a marriage that has been dissolved in God's sight. If a man marries a scripturally divorced woman, or vice versa, if they are committing any sin, that sin is not adultery.

Interpreting in Context

It should be obvious to everyone that a specific application of Jesus' teaching on divorce is subject to

an initial presumption of context. When we assume
that Jesus is contrasting the teachings of Moses to an
immature culture with his own laws for his approaching kingdom, we come up with a different set of
answers than when we assume that he is addressing
the problem of interpreting Moses' teaching on the
subject to the Jews living under the Jewish age. Still
others argue logically that Jesus' teaching was limited to the time in which it was given and that his
law for the Christian age, stated clearly by Paul in
1 Corinthians 7:39, allows no grounds whatever for
divorce, even sexual immorality.

Those skilled in exegesis, or critical interpretation, have always been, and still remain, at variance
over exactly what is or is not bound upon Christians.
So how fair is it to expect the average Christian,
unskilled in biblical languages, Jewish backgrounds,
and principles of hermeneutics, or interpretation, to
arrive at a clear answer? The traditional answer is:
It is better to be safe than sorry.

But how safe is it to take a stringent and judgmental position and use it to bind our opinion or
interpretation on someone else? Or worse, how safe
is it to use our position as grounds to disfellowship
or withdraw from someone? These actions far more
often result in permanent estrangement from the
church rather than in restoration to fellowship,
which is God's desire.

No Pat Answer

It is unproductive to impose one possible interpretation, whether it represents the view of a minority or a majority, upon people who do not agree with
it and to use it as a test of fellowship. Certainly,
honesty and fairness should keep us from deciding

on a pat answer to a question when the issue's linguistic and historical parameters are not (and perhaps can never be) precisely fixed. Dialogue and further study should always be left open. As long as doubt persists, room for differing views should be allowed. Integrity requires us to base our response to every moral and doctrinal question on the Scriptures. However, we can't impose a conviction rooted in interpretation upon Christians who can't honestly share that conviction. "Therefore let us stop passing judgment on one another. Instead, make up your mind not to put any stumbling block or obstacle in your brother's way" (Romans 14:13). Since love is not self-seeking, love does not force its opinions on others. The only person you can bind such strict interpretation on is yourself.

Then there is the added complication that occurs when you consider the children of a shaky marriage. The question is, whose rights are to be ignored— those of the betrayed spouse or those of the children? Children are the innocent victims of parents' sins. But to say that rectifying the sin of adultery should take priority over the consequences to the children does not really cope with the social and moral problems involved. It is a case where strict adherence to law (if indeed any law applies) appears to violate other legitimate human interests and moral values. We are faced with a dilemma. Do we terminate a marriage and sacrifice the right of the children to a normal home and parents? Or do we respond as Jesus did to the adulterous woman: "Neither do I condemn you; go and sin no more" (John 8:11, NKJV).

Of course there are those who say that adultery still persists even after the original mates have long since remarried and had families. These people would say that Jesus' statement would require dissolving both marriages and either restoring the failed marriage or remaining single.

Jewish authorities calculate that about 30 percent of Jewish marriages on the average have ended in divorce through the last two thousand years. If so, there must have been thousands of divorced persons in Peter's audience in Acts 2. It is curious that he did not exclude them from the invitation to be baptized. He commanded them to repent, but a divorced Jew would not have had any consciousness of sin in regard to his marriage. In fact, Paul's admonition to avoid sexual immorality by getting married would appear, practically speaking, to relate particularly to one whose weakness to sexual temptation had destroyed his marriage in the first place.

Clear-cut answers to the problem of failed marriages are not easy to come by. In the first place, branding one partner as "the guilty party" is most often an extreme oversimplification. Every marriage counselor is well aware that a divorce situation is rarely so straightforward that the real aggressor against the marriage can be identified. Most generally both parties must share the blame for the collapse of the marriage. Self-giving love must be offered by both partners for a marriage to be truly successful. The real source of the problem (even in cases of adultery) may even be the failure of "the innocent party" to fulfill his (her) marital obligations. Before positive aggression (adultery) against the marriage occurred, the marriage may have been doomed to failure by negative aggression from the other partner.

Only God Knows

How people handle these perplexing situations will depend upon their orientation. Some will argue that complicating factors do not alter the clear legal position under consideration. Others will state the principle of "the sabbath was made for man, not man for the sabbath." They will take the position that every biblical principle comes from God's desire to promote human good and happiness. And the strict application of a general principle of law (such as "thou shalt not kill") which does not promote human good and happiness is a violation of God's will. One holds that the principle behind a law of God and the structure of the law are inseparable and not subject to change in any situation. The other holds that God's laws are rooted in their intended objectives and are a means to a desirable end; when the context changes so that the desirable end is not realized, then obeying that law becomes counterproductive and does not have God's blessing.

Who Is Right?

Who is right? Each is right in trying to protect what he believes is the primary interest of truth. Each presents internal contradictions which seem beyond human intelligence to resolve. If the answers were as obvious and straightforward as simplistic solutions suggest, the problems would not have vexed the minds of church leaders throughout the Christian age. It's only in loving each other unselfishly, the way God loves us, being self-giving rather than self-seeking, that we can come closest to understanding God's will for us. But, in the final analysis, only the Divine intelligence knows the ultimate answers. Until he reveals the absolute answer to us, we must love and support one another through difficult and uncertain times.

Focusing Your Faith

1. In what ways do careers place stress on today's marriages? How can a church help ease the tension? How can you help?

2. If your church's role in families were that of physician rather than judge, how could that change the way divorced people are treated?

3. What prescriptions would you recommend for newlyweds? For couples with marital problems?

4. With the increasing divorce rate, what can your church do to minister to the children of divorce?

5. If Moses' law and Jesus' teachings are clear about marriage and divorce, why can't we as Christians know God's will in every situation?

6. What can a church do to strengthen the marriage of a Christian to an unbeliever?

7. Think of a situation in which you acted in a self-seeking way. What were the consequences? What would you do differently?

1 Corinthians 9:19-21

Though I am free and belong to no man, I make myself a slave to everyone, to win as many as possible. To the Jews I became like a Jew, to win the Jews. To those under the law I became like one under the law (though I myself am not under the law), so as to win those under the law. To those not having the law I became like one not having the law (though I am not free from God's law but am under Christ's law), so as to win those not having the law.

Chapter 7

Breaking
the Law of Love

1 Corinthians 9:19-21

Once while living in a two-roomed, thatch-roofed hut in Sinde Mission in Zambia, I hired a young African man named Joseph to help me around the house. Besides cooking my meals, he made my

The Way:

Love always trusts.

1 Corinthians 13:7

morning tea, washed and ironed my clothes, and generally kept everything spic-and-span. Joseph served up some weird and wonderful foods: some out of my pantry, some that he bargained for in the villages. I began a practice with Joseph, which I maintained through the years, of leaving small amounts of change so that he could buy eggs, chickens, and other produce from peddlers. Many of the older missionaries thought it was both foolish and unfair to subject an employee to an open invitation

to steal. Throughout the years, however, I was never
taken advantage of, whereas some of the more
prudent householders were bothered with constant
pilfering. Europeans, including most missionaries,
kept the sugar in a locked cupboard, and the house-
wife carried the key on her person. When the tea
was served the young man was allowed to unlock the
cupboard until the tea service was over. I took the
opposite tack. When I hired someone new to help me
in the house, I showed him the sugar canister and
told him, "You are welcome to make tea for yourself
and stir in all the sugar you want." I don't know how
much sugar was lost as a consequence over the
years, but since I never noticed the difference, it
certainly didn't hurt me significantly. It saved a lot
of bother in locking and unlocking cupboards. And
because of our mutual trust, a long-lasting friendship developed.[1]

"Love always trusts," Paul told the Corinthians.
It's because Christ freed us from a law of sin and
death that we are able to trust him with our very
souls. And by loving and trusting others, we're able
to express our love and trust in Jesus.

Paul introduces two subjects in chapter 9: situation ethics and law as it relates to the Christian.

Situation Ethics

The term situation ethics has picked up a bad
connotation because it has been used to justify a
code of conduct based on sheer expediency at the
expense of basic principles. The term itself, however,
means merely a course of behavior suitable to each
given situation. As we go through life, we have
innumerable opportunities to influence others favorably or unfavorably, to make their lives brighter or

to inflict misery upon them. Often, it's what we don't do that offends people, rather than what we actually say or do.

People who pride themselves on being "brutally honest" are in reality branding themselves as being arrogant and uncaring. Especially when dealing with cultural differences, unnecessary and ill-considered frankness can build walls that may never be torn down. Proverbs 18:19 puts it well: "An offended brother is more unyielding than a fortified city, and disputes are like the barred gates of a citadel." This directly applies to relating to people's culture and background in order to teach them the gospel.

Because of his experience and training, Paul was able to cross freely from one culture to another. He had been brought up in the bustling Gentile city of Tarsus and was a tentmaker, a profession that brought him in contact with virtually every race in the Middle East. So he was at ease with both Greek philosophers and Armenian traders. He had an excellent education in Hellenistic literature. He had the language training to enable him to shift from the common (*koine*) Greek in which he wrote, and which was the world language of his day, to the more sophisticated Attic Greek when he addressed the philosophers of Athens. The Greeks trusted him because he was one of them. Yet, he could throw off his Gentile cover like an old coat and become a "Hebrew of Hebrews" (Philippians 3:5) when the situation required it. So, likewise, the Jews trusted him because he was one of them.

Jew to the Jew

We do not know the specifics of Paul's early life, but we know from brief references in the Scriptures that his Jewish qualifications were impeccable. He

obviously had attained a position of responsible rank
in the hierarchy in Jerusalem (Acts 7:58-8:1; 9:1, 2).
He was trained in the Law by Gamaliel, the ranking
Jewish educator of his day (and one of only a half-
dozen Jewish teachers who received the title of
Prince [*Nasi*] for his great learning). To be a gradu-
ate of Gamaliel's training was the first-century
equivalent of a Ph.D. in biblical studies.

When situation ethics violated a principle of truth, Paul took a public, even though unpopular, stand against it.

Paul had no problems with keeping the institutions of Judaism (Acts 16:3; 20:16) and even its
rituals (Acts 21:17-24), so long as they were considered customary and were not bound upon Christians. For instance, Paul would never have done
ordinary work on a Sabbath for fear that he might
offend the Jews (Romans 14:5). And he certainly
didn't object to eating meat that had been offered to
an idol, provided that it did not become an issue
(1 Corinthians 8:4-13; 10:27-33). But he believed
that exercising his freedom of choice in such a matter should never be allowed to harm his Christian
influence. Circumcision was a matter of indifference
unless it was bound as a religious obligation (1 Corinthians 7:19; Galatians 2:3-5), in which case he
vehemently opposed it (Galatians 5:2-4). However, in
line with his avowed policy of trying to "please
everybody in every way" (1 Corinthians 10:33) he
circumcised Timothy (Acts 16:3) to make him more
acceptable to the Jews.

When situation ethics violated a principle of
truth, Paul took a public, even though unpopular,
stand against it (Galatians 2:11-13).

There were times when Paul's Jewish credentials gave him an advantage. Paul did not hesitate to flash his high standing in orthodox Judaism when the occasion required it (Acts 22:1-5). He and Barnabas were able to enter freely into Jewish synagogues and accept invitations to address the assembly, an opportunity that certainly would not have been extended to them had they not been accepted as practicing Jews (Acts 13:15; 14:1).

Non-Jew to the Non-Jew

Although they are often highly esteemed as individuals, Jews have rarely been popular as a race in Gentile countries. Some say it is because of their sharp business practices, but probably the principal reason is their different culture, morals, and religious practices (Esther 3:8). For whatever reasons, it was difficult for one easily recognized as a Jew to gain the attention of Gentile audiences. Familiarity with the writings of Moses carried no weight with followers of Greek philosophers such as Plato and Epictetus.

No doubt Paul's flexibility and ability to gain people's trust were compelling reasons why the Lord chose Paul, the genius from Tarsus, as his apostle to the Gentile world. He was able to shift easily from a discussion of the Torah in a synagogue to disputing with Greek philosophers in the public square (Acts 17:17, 18). He would never have offended a Jewish audience by references to great Gentile teachers, but he quoted Greek poets in the course of addressing the Athenians (Acts 17:28). When preaching to a synagogue audience, Paul started his sermon with the captivity of the Israelites in Egypt (Acts 13:17). But when addressing a Greek audience, he began with an altar to an unknown God (Acts 17:22). His great learning impressed even a Roman governor (Acts 26:24), but he became a humble gatherer of firewood with Maltese peasants (Acts 28:1-3). Who among the apostles except Paul could actually have started a congregation among Nero's elite Praetorian guard (Philippians 4:22)? He used his Roman citizenship to back down meddlesome magistrates (Acts 16:37-39) and to protect his own rights (Acts 22:23-29). He again employed it to remove himself from the jurisdiction of the Jewish court by appealing directly to Caesar (Acts 25:9-12).

Practical Lessons

What practical lessons may we learn from the determination of Paul "to become all things to all men"? After all, he was probably the most successful evangelist in the history of the world (1 Corinthians 15:10; Colossians 1:23) so his choice of adapting to the sensitivities of others must have been correct.

We should seek understanding and not confrontation.

---

1. We should seek understanding and not confrontation. Jesus said, "The people of this world are more shrewd in dealing with their own kind than are the people of the light" (Luke 16:8). A salesman cannot sell his product if he antagonizes, bullies, or belittles a prospect. All too often Christians have opportunities closed in their faces, not because of their beliefs but because of their belligerence in pushing those beliefs upon others. If only they knew that winning an argument often means losing a soul. An insurance salesman knows better than to insult the intelligence of a potential customer. He is very careful to first build as many points of harmony as possible before encouraging the prospect to make a decision. He knows full well that the person will not buy his policy if he distrusts him or dislikes him personally. If a person of the business world, with no greater aim than to gain a policyholder, goes to such pains to establish rapport and trust with a potential client, how much more effort should a Christian make to favorably impress a person he hopes to win for eternal life? The successful businessperson takes no comfort from having "told it like it is" if the result is an offended prospect. It is more important to lead a soul to Jesus than to prove how right we are.

> *It is more important to lead a soul to Jesus than to prove how right we are.*

2. *We should remember that we are not working for ourselves—we are ambassadors for Christ* (2 Corinthians 5:20). Ambassadors must be able to redirect their own interests and feelings to the cause they represent. They do not criticize the cultural peculiarities or social codes of the host country. They tolerate the insults and bad manners of others with graciousness, knowing that allowing themselves to respond in the same way might jeopardize their mission. They are trusting, patient, and considerate because they know that their own egos must never get in the way of effectively serving the interests of their own country—a country to which they will one day return to give an account of their stewardship.

Sibaliki, the African son of one of the church members at Sinde, once accompanied me to a mission station eighty miles away in Kalomo. He was good natured, so we got along very well for the four years he worked for me there. On a trip to a distant village, he fell in love with a beautiful young woman.

"She's *very* fat," he proudly announced. But marrying a bride from a distant tribe created some unusual cultural problems. After overcoming difficult financial negotiations for his bride, Sibaliki realized that this was not the end of his struggles. It seemed that some of their customs were very troublesome. "One of the worst was that members of the bride's clan congratulate the bridegroom by pulling his nose," he told me. "I thought I wasn't going to have any nose left!" Another custom was that the mother-in-law could call on her daughter's husband at any time to work in her field. "Someone's coming" meant his wife's mother was on his trail and he'd better run.

Despite the unusual customs, Sibaliki remained patient and trustworthy and endured nosepulling rather than risk insulting his new bride's family. We should be so tolerant as we seek to bring others to Christ.

What honor and dignity has been placed upon us! We have been appointed personal ambassadors of the King of kings! But what an awesome responsibility goes with it! Not only must we accept the challenge of communicating God's grace to a world without hope, but we must do it in such a way that causes as little offense as possible. Paul admonishes us: "Do not cause anyone to stumble, whether Jews, Greeks or the church of God" (1 Corinthians 10:32). We are not likely to cause offense unnecessarily if we live by his rule: "I make myself a slave to everyone, to win as many as possible" (9:19b).

3. We should avoid making major issues out of minor, peripheral matters. If a person is lost, it is because he has not experienced the mercy of God mediated by the shed blood of Jesus Christ, not because of what he calls his church or his church leaders. The requirements for membership in Christ's one spiritual body and for receiving God's spirit are simple and unequivocal: one Lord, one faith, one baptism (Ephesians 4:4, 5). If anyone has trusted Jesus as Lord and Master, has espoused the one faith, and has been born into the kingdom by the one baptism, that person is a child of God and the brother or sister of every other Christian on earth. There may still be many areas where the faith of new Christians is immature, and my responsibility to teach and nurture them never stops as long as they need my help. As a matter of fact, minor points of disagreement generally fall away or solve themselves once a person has committed his life to Christ in baptism. It is a tragic mistake to ridicule others' beliefs and make them feel foolish. We may very well be shutting the door of the kingdom against them.

We certainly have to oppose errors that prevent someone from becoming obedient to the faith, but we must do it tactfully, lovingly, and with respect for their dignity.

4. People learn more by watching our example than by listening to our words. Educators know by experience that the eye is an effective learning organ. Often a simple demonstration is more effective in communicating a concept than hours of lecturing. What we hear is important and is an indispensable part of the learning process, but what we see and hear is more likely to be vividly remembered. That suggests that there is much more to communicating the gospel than simply speaking words. Jesus said that others will be brought to glorify our heavenly Father when they see our good deeds (Matthew 5:16). Jesus' criticism of the Pharisees as teachers was that their behavior was inconsistent with their preaching (Matthew 23:2-4). If unbelievers perceive the church to be a judgmental, backbiting, self-centered group of fanatics, we can advertise Christianity through mass media and newspapers and preach on street corners, but we will not be successful in reaching the community. If they observe us to be a caring community of happy activists, intent upon leaving the world a little better place than we found it, and offering them hope both in this life and the life to come, they will seek us out.

Law

A question the Corinthians had was, Which law was in effect? In the first place, God has always had laws with respect to people's behavior. Romans 4:15 says, "where there is no law there is no transgression." Yet Galatians 3:19 tells us that the Mosaic code "was added because of transgressions." This confirms that God's law was in effect before Moses; otherwise, there could have been no transgression.

In Paul's own case, the Jewish law was the law of Moses which encoded God's eternal moral principles. It was a disciplinary measure to prepare a special people for the coming of the Messiah. In the case of the Gentile Romans, it was God's eternal law that "the soul who sins is the one who will die." "Death came to all men, because all sinned" (Romans 5:12). Even in cultures where they had no written code by which to judge morality, the requirements of God's law were written in their hearts and consciences (Romans 2:15). The Jews were accustomed to and wanted a clearly defined written set of laws. The Gentiles had God's law written only in their hearts and consciences. So how did Paul explain Christ's law so that both Jews and Gentiles could comprehend and accept it?

What Law Is the Christian Under?

"I am not free from God's law but am under Christ's law" (1 Corinthians 9:21). A literal translation of the original would be: "Not being lawless [with respect] of God, but *in* a law of Christ." Paul is making the point that because Christians are not under a legal code, we are not, therefore, law-less— we still have behavioral guidelines. There is a law of Christ which holds us in a saved relationship to God. James calls it the "royal law found in Scripture, 'Love your neighbor as yourself' " (James 2:8). It is "the perfect law that gives freedom" and is the law that forms the basis on which we are judged (James 1:25; 2:12).

"My command is this: Love each other as I have loved you" (John 15:12).

Jesus said that the commandment to love God and people comprises the whole essence of the law (Matthew 22:36-40). If we truly love and trust our God and our neighbor, all other commandments are inclusive. Jesus summed up his commandments to his disciples by saying, "My command is this: Love each other as I have loved you" (John 15:12). In Romans 13:8b, 9 Paul adds, "For he who loves his fellowman has fulfilled the law. The commandments, 'Do not commit adultery,' 'Do not murder,' 'Do not steal,' 'Do not covet,' and whatever other commandment there may be, are summed up in this one rule: 'Love your neighbor as yourself.' " Paul takes his explanation further by saying, "Love does no harm to its neighbor. Therefore love is the fulfillment of the law" (v. 10). Actually, in the Greek the passage does not have the definite article "the." It should read:

"Therefore, love is the fulfillment of law"—all law, not just the Mosaic code.

In Christ's Law

The argument sometimes is made that the cross of Jesus brought an end to the law of Moses ("He took it away, nailing it to the cross" Colossians 2:14). In its place Christ instituted his *own* law, which is also God's law for our time. We are, therefore, still under law, but it is Christ's law, not Moses' law. This is a simplistic view, and it is not what the apostle is saying.

It is important to note that Paul does not actually say that he was *under* Christ's law (*hupo nomon*), but "*in* a law of Christ" (*ennomos*). He distinguishes between the situation of "those under the law" (*hupo nomon*) and the situation of Christians who are *in* a law of Christ. "We are not under *law* but under grace" (Romans 6:15). Paul means we are not under any law; if the law of Moses was meant, he would have used the article, *the law.* "It is because through Christ the law of the Spirit of life set me free from the law of sin and death" (Romans 8:2). A better translation is: "The Spirit's law of life in Christ Jesus set me free from the law of sin and death." In other words, the Spirit's law says that those who are alive in Jesus Christ are no longer subject to a legal code.

The real purpose of law is to compel law breakers to show respect for the rights of others. As Christians we shouldn't need a law to make us respect others' rights. A Christian's code of behavior is motivated by love, and, therefore, so far exceeds the requirements of law that the law itself becomes irrelevant. To illustrate this principle: A loving father may be dimly aware that there are laws in his state setting minimum requirements for the care of his children, but he has no interest in those laws. They are so far below the special care he will give his children that state guidelines do not concern him. Only if he stopped loving his children and started abusing them would the law relate to him at all. Or, take the situation of the jet pilot flying at nearly forty thousand feet above sea level. Below him are giant boulders, cliffs, and forests that could dash his plane to pieces in an instant. But his mind is not on those remote hazards on the ground. It is fixed upon reaching his destination. If he should descend to hilltop level, he would immediately become concerned about missing the objects looming in front of him. But as long as he maintains his altitude, those far-off obstacles pose no threat at all.

The Colossians, distracted by the obstacles in their way, were tempted to return to the law of Moses (and to the numerous human regulations that had been derived from it) "just in case" they might not be good enough. Paul exclaims, "Since you died with Christ to the basic principles of this world, why, as though you still belonged to it, do you submit to its rules: 'Do not handle! Do not taste! Do not touch!'?" (Colossians 2:20, 21).

Paul is asking, "Now that you have been made alive in Christ and are constrained by his love to walk in his steps, why would you want to go back to the ABCs of human morality and ethics?" And, indeed, it is a very valid question, not just for the Colossian brethren, but for immature Christians of every age. The fact is, many are at least nominally Christians, but their lives are not fully committed to following Christ, and they feel more comfortable with laws to regulate their behavior. They regard themselves as potential transgressors because they practice spiritual brinkmanship, coming as close as they dare to what they perceive to be the minimum standards without actually crossing the line. They want their "duty" spelled out in black and white, and so they ask questions like: "Do I have to give a tenth of my income? Do I have to take the Lord's Supper every Sunday? Do I have to attend church when I'm on my vacation?"

Let's take as an example the fact that God once required his people to tithe. God expected every person in spiritual infancy to return one tenth of his income to him. Therefore, we might logically assume that God would expect every Christian of average income and expenses to give him one-tenth as a starting point, the bottom rung of the ladder. But that is only a basic principle. As the Christian matures, he will certainly increase that ratio until finally he has no interest in percentage at all. He will come to realize that everything he has belongs to God and that he is simply God's manager. He knows that all of it must be dedicated to God's will, and that what he spends on his children's shoes (yes, and on recreation, too) is as much given to the Lord as what he puts in the collection plate. But this "honor system" is based upon love for God and people, and it will not work for the member who is still in the swaddling clothes of his relationship with Christ. Until he learns to let go he must have the discipline of percentage giving.

The one who asks, "Do I have to take communion every week?" belongs in one of two categories: (1) the beginning Christian who is still feeling his way toward what God expects of him, or (2) the opportunist who wants to buy salvation at the cheapest possible price. Such a person probably never does actually commune with the Lord and never shall until he is truly converted. Instead of a thanksgiving (*eucharist*), it becomes an insult. As with other practices, the Lord's Supper has no real meaning when it is reduced to a burdensome, legal duty.

Grace vs. Law

Certainly nothing Paul taught on the Christian's freedom from law was intended to imply that Christians can be freethinking libertines—quite the opposite. The Christian is born again to a life resurrected from death. He is guided by a new motivation—"want to" instead of "have to." Paul asked the Romans: "What shall we say, then? Shall we go on sinning so that grace may increase? By no means! We died to sin; how can we live in it any longer?" (Romans 6:1, 2). Christians have the guiding influence of the Holy Spirit which constrains us to ignore minimum standards of law and strive to conform to the likeness of God's Son (Romans 8:29).

Law, as such, is no longer relevant for the Christian. "We also know that law is made not for the righteous but for lawbreakers and rebels, the ungodly and sinful, the unholy and irreligious; for those who kill their fathers or mothers, for murderers, for adulterers and perverts, for slave traders and liars and perjurers—and for whatever else is contrary to the sound doctrine that conforms to the glorious gospel of the blessed God, which he entrusted to me" (1 Timothy 1:9-11).

Grace is no license to sin. "Christ is the end of law" for righteousness, not sin (Romans 10:4; note that in the original text there is no article *the* before *law*). For those who are not led by the Spirit, God's eternal law of sin and death (not the Mosaic law), is still very much in effect.

Principally, when Paul argues the contrast between righteousness by grace and by law, he is talking about law as a concept, although he often designates the Mosaic law as a prime example. Of the more than 120 times the apostle refers to law, less than half are referring specifically to the law of Moses. To draw the conclusion that Paul was simply contending that the law of Moses had passed away, and that Christians are now under a new set of laws, is to miss entirely the thrust of his argument.

We entrust our souls to him; he entrusts his grace to us.

Christians are *free* from law—free to be all we can be in Jesus Christ through the indwelling of God's Spirit. Now that we know God and are known of God, we have no desire to be enslaved by "those weak and miserable principles" of a legal code (Galatians 4:9). We can now "risk" becoming all things to all people in order to win them to Christ.

Thanks be to God for his redeeming grace which has made us free from a law of sin and death! Because Christ paid the price, we do not have to tremble under some exacting point system with our salvation always teetering on a knife-edge. We entrust our souls to him; he entrusts his grace to us, knowing that as long as we love him we will not abuse that trust. He loved us enough to die for us. We love him enough to live for him and, if need be, even die for him. "Love always trusts."

Notes:

[1] Eldred Echols, *Wings of the Morning: The Saga of an African Pilgrim* (Fort Worth: Wings Press, 1989).

Focusing Your Faith

1. What person do you trust most in your life? What trustworthy traits does he or she possess?

2. What "baggage" do you carry in your life that makes it difficult for you to trust others? How has that affected your capacity to trust God?

3. What "unpopular" groups of people in your community is your church an ambassador to: homeless or poor people? Drug and alcohol abusers? AIDS patients? Unwed mothers?

4. When we are tolerant of views that differ from our own, what do we risk? What do we risk when we are intolerant?

5. How do the Scriptures about our not being "under law" affect your views about your salvation? About grace? About freedom?

6. What are some ways you believe we have made major issues out of minor matters? What has been the results of that?

7. Paul went to the temple and participated in Jewish vows and rituals. How would your church view someone's actions if they did that today?

1 Corinthians 10:21

*You cannot drink the cup of the Lord
and the cup of demons too; you cannot have
a part in both the Lord's table and the table
of demons.*

Chapter 8

Flirting
with Demons

1 Corinthians 10:14-33

Paul warned the Corinthians against "eating with" Christians who were living in open sin (1 Corinthians 5:11). Throughout history in most cultures taking a meal with someone has signified friendship

> ## The Way:
>
> *Love does not delight in evil.*
>
> *1 Corinthians 13:6*

between the two persons. This is probably the basis for God's command to the young Judaen prophet (1 Kings 13) not to eat bread or drink water in Bethel when he went there to denounce the corruption of Jeroboam.

To eat with the idolaters of northern Israel was to appear to condone their sins. Unfortunately for the young prophet, he listened to a lying prophet of Bethel who told him that God had revealed to him that the visitor should eat at his table. The young man did so and lost his life to a lion the Lord sent to meet him on the way home.

Eating at "the table of demons" is still literally a great problem in largely pagan societies. Such a problem arose in a village congregation in Zambia. A prominent heathen had died, and, according to the funeral customs of his traditional beliefs, family members slaughtered and cooked a number of oxen to eat in honor of their ancestral spirits. There were dissenting opinions over whether Christians should go. Some of the younger Christians wanted to go and participate in the feast, obviously to show respect to the deceased, but also because it was an opportunity to fill themselves on beef, a rare commodity in their diet. "You shouldn't eat that meat!" the elders of the church cautioned them. "But we don't believe in the mizimo (ancestral spirits) and our pagan friends know we don't; it's only meat," they protested. "Besides, it will be an insult to the relatives of the deceased not to eat." "It is only meat to you," the elders said, "but to them it is worship. If you eat it, they'll regard you as participating in heathen worship." That occurred years ago, and it is very possible that a new generation of elders would today render a different decision.

Satan's Agents

A demon is by general definition a malicious spirit who is one of Satan's agents in working harm to human beings. The word means no more than a lesser god, whether good or evil, and was used in reference to the whole pantheon of pagan gods. In the New Testament, however, it is used only in the evil sense, usually in the diminutive (a little devil). It is never used of Satan (the word for *devil* in passages referring to him is *diabolos*—the accuser). The

existence of unclean spirits, or demons, is fully
attested in the New Testament writings (mostly in
the Gospels). Deafness, dumbness, insanity, epi-
lepsy, and many other afflictions were attributed to
the presence of demons. Paul himself exorcised a
spirit of Python (clairvoyance) and many other evil
spirits (Acts 16:16; 19:12).

Paul does not mean to imply by calling them
"demons" that the pagan gods had personal existence, for he has just asked in 1 Corinthians 10:19,
"Do I mean then that a sacrifice offered to an idol is
anything, or that an idol is anything? No." They
nevertheless had whatever power their worshipers
believed them to have and therefore exerted a tre-
mendous influence for evil in blinding people's minds
to the true God. They were indeed demons, agents
through whom Satan separated people from God.

Keep Your Distance

God foresaw that association with idolatry in any
form would seduce Israel away from their faithful-
ness to him: "Be careful not to make a treaty with
those who live in the land; for when they prostitute
themselves to their gods and sacrifice to them, they
will invite you and you will eat their sacrifices. And
when you choose some of their daughters as wives
for your sons and those daughters prostitute themselves to their gods, they will lead your sons to do
the same" (Exodus 34:15, 16).

God was saying, in effect: Keep your distance
from idolatry and idolaters. If you once relax your
guard, one thing will lead to another. Presently you
will be intermarrying with them, and your descendants will be idolaters. The Hebrews ignored that
warning to their great cost. Esau married Hittite
women, and his descendants, the Edomites, were

idolaters. Solomon forsook God's command,
and "his wives turned his heart after other gods"
(1 Kings 11:4), and he is not among the great heroes
of the faith named in Hebrews chapter 11. Ahab
married Jezebel, a Phoenician princess (1 Kings
16:31), and she led him and most of Israel to forsake
the Lord and worship Baal.

We should not test the Lord's patience as did
some of the Israelites (1 Corinthians 10:7). We
should try only to please our Savior who chose not to
please himself but chose rather to endure humiliation for our sakes. Some of the Corinthian Christians
were practicing spiritual brinkmanship, trying to
maintain a relationship with Christ and at the same
time still engaging in worldly practices that they
should have left behind forever. A form of Christianity that seeks to find the rim of Satan's realm without tumbling in is, at best, immature and untaught.
At worst, it is completely fraudulent. We cannot
survive in this age's wilderness of sin and ever hope
to reach that Canaan of promise if we are forever
weeping over the leeks and garlic of Egypt. Rather
we will set our minds on things above, not on earthly
things (Colosians 3:2). Then there will be no temptation to "delight in evil" or see how far we can venture
beyond the things of Christ without losing our
influence and perhaps our souls.

Paul warned the Corinthians not to be "yoked
together with unbelievers" (2 Corinthians 6:14), and
the principle is still valid. In marriage, the closest
union in earthly life, it is most important to choose a
mate that shares your spiritual values.

In fairness, it's true that committed Christians
often convert their non-Christian mates. Statistics
show that a quarter of the non-Christian partners
become Christians, a quarter of the Christian mates

go to their husband's (or wife's) religion, and in the remaining 50 percent both husband and wife drift away from any religion at all or remain religiously divided throughout the marriage. While such marriages are ill-advised, they are perfectly valid in the sight of God. The Christian partner in the marriage should receive all the encouragement possible and be assured of the congregation's love and support. A major consideration is that the children born to such a marriage not be left without spiritual guidance and Christian fellowship.

Pagan Tables

Tables in pagan temples were often objects of great value and beauty. We do not have specific information about the tables in the great temples of Corinth, but they would surely have been spectacular. Diodorus (first century B.C.) described a table in the temple of Bel as being of beaten gold forty-five feet long and fifteen feet wide. However, the splendor of the tables was not a factor in the problem over idols at Corinth.

The staff of a pagan temple not only offered animal sacrifices on behalf of their followers, they also sold the offered meat later to the public. It could either be bought and cooked at home, or it could be purchased already prepared for eating in the temple restaurants. The pagan priests were the caterers of ancient times. A large temple would have public rooms that could be hired for social occasions with the food supplied from the temple kitchens. That put many Christians in a dilemma: whether to accept an invitation from a friend to attend such a function and risk being thought an idolater or refuse and insult the friend. An ancient papyrus preserves such an invitation: "Chareimon invites you to dine at the

table of the Lord Serapis." From the same period a
fragment of an invitation has been found from one
Roman to another inviting him to attend the engage-
ment party for his daughter "in the supper room in
the Temple of Apollo."

Some of the Corinthian Christians argued like
this: "We are Christians, and we know that the
pagan gods are imaginary. Meat offered to them is
just that—meat—no different from other meat. Our
Christian freedom allows us to choose whether to
accept or decline an invitation to a social function in
an idol's temple."

Paul responds: "Food does not bring us near to
God; we are no worse if we do not eat, and no better
if we do. Be careful, however, that the exercise of
your freedom does not become a stumbling block to
the weak. For if anyone with a weak conscience sees
you who have this knowledge eating in an idol's
temple, won't he be emboldened to eat what has
been sacrificed to idols? So this weak brother, for
whom Christ died, is destroyed by your knowledge.
When you sin against your brothers in this way and
wound their weak conscience, you sin against Christ.
Therefore, if what I eat causes my brother to fall into
sin, I will never eat meat again, so that I will not
cause him to fall" (1 Corinthians 8:8-13).

Dangers of Eating in an Idol's Temple

There were three inherent dangers in eating
meat at a pagan temple:

*1. The Christian ran the risk of again becoming
entrapped in actual idol worship.* This posed a far
greater possibility of regression into the old way of
life than the Corinthians appear to have realized.
Invisible scars remain even after the sinner has

turned away from the sinful life. A reformed alcoholic cannot dare to touch a drink in the assumption that he is now free from its influence. A former compulsive gambler cannot place the smallest bet without awakening the old demon.

I was once discussing with a wise African teacher the fact that so many African Christians continue to participate in pagan rituals to varying degrees. "What you have to realize," he observed, "is that you convert the grandchildren. To illustrate my point, my father is the first generation of my family to become a Christian. He sincerely believed in Jesus Christ, but he also believed in the power of the ancestral spirits. I know with my mind that they are nothing, and yet I am still careful not to violate the ancient taboos, just in case. But my son is free from the old superstitions. They have no hold over him at all. He is completely Christian."

The Corinthian Christians, who had to prove to themselves and to others that they were now free from the hold of idols by eating their sacrifices, were placing their souls at great risk.

Paul invites them to remember Israel's tragic mistake in flirting with evil idolatry. He is probably alluding to the event recorded in Numbers 25 during the wilderness wanderings. Israelite men were seduced by Moabite women and were led to eat sacrifices to their idols and even to bow down before the images. As a result, 24,000 Israelites were destroyed by a plague. In Corinth also, sacred prostitution was a part of pagan worship. The Temple of Venus had one thousand free prostitutes. This posed a problem for the Corinthian church, and it is reflected by Paul's words in 1 Corinthians 6:15, 16: "Do you not know that your bodies are members of Christ himself? Shall I then take the members of

Christ and unite them with a prostitute? Never! Do you not know that he who unites himself with a prostitute is one with her in body? For it is said, 'The two will become one flesh.' "

2. *A strong Christian had a responsibility to newer Christians.* Even if a Christian could eat the sacrifices without any of the old fear of the pagan god being aroused, he shouldn't expose the newer Christians to what was for them a deadly peril. By following in his footsteps they might again become victims of the old delusion.

3. *Christians might compromise their influence among the pagans whom they had a responsibility to evangelize.* A pagan friend who attended the Sunday assembly with a Corinthian Christian but who on Thursday saw that Christian eating at the Temple of Venus would have his confidence in the integrity of the Christian shaken. His response would likely be, "That hypocrite! Telling me how wrong it is to eat the sacrifices to the gods, and then doing the same thing!"

The Old Man

Christianity is often only a thin veneer over the lives of converts from paganism. They learn to say the right things and to wear the outer trappings of piety, but all too often the "old man" is lurking just under the surface and ready to come out again when they return to their pagan environment. That is not to say that they are insincere when they accept Christianity. It is just that they are convinced intellectually but not emotionally. Sometimes they project this ambivalence in their own religious lives onto their perception of their missionary teachers. In other words, they feel that we also have skeletons in the closet from our own religious past that we may secretly bring out from time to time.

An interesting example of this occurred while I was teaching at Namwianga Mission in Zambia. As everyone knows, Americans are addicted to cookouts or "weenie roasts," especially if there is an obvious excuse for having them, such as the Fourth of July. When that particular holiday came up, the American community at Namwianga decided to celebrate the occasion with a weenie roast in the late evening. It had to be outside, of course, to be a real weenie roast, but the after-dark hours in those parts belonged to the various varmints and snakes that inhabit the African bush and come out at night. We preferred a place where, even in the moonlight, we could see a cobra before he was in striking distance, so we chose a granite "kopie," a low hill with a flat top of bare granite. On this we built our bonfire, and when it had subsided somewhat we toasted our weiners and marshmallows and sang songs until the fire burned low and the night grew chilly.

The following day the African students were sullen and aloof and would not look at us directly—a sure sign that something was seriously awry. I finally accosted one of the young men directly: "Alright, out with it! What are you all angry about?" "Oh, we aren't angry," he replied quickly. "We are just disappointed to find that our missionaries are such hypocrites!" That was a fairly serious charge, so I pressed him, "What have we done that is so hypocritical?"

"Have you not taught us that we should give up our spirit worship?" he asked. "We have indeed," I responded, "but how is that connected with the cold, silent treatment you are giving us?"

"Have you not told us that building fires on the hilltops to our rain god is idolatry?" he went on.

"Yes, we have."

"And yet you are guilty of the same thing!" he accused.

I stared at him as one looks at a person who has just taken leave of his senses. "When have we ever worshiped a rain god?" I demanded.

"You were seen when you left your houses last night and gathered and worshiped around the fire on a hilltop."

I was very relieved at this twist in the conversation. "Oh, that!" I said, laughing. "We just went out on the hilltop to cook our food and sing awhile. It's our custom."

Now he was beginning to get angry. "We are not children, that you can satisfy us with little stories!" he explained indignantly. "Do you expect us to believe that people who have stoves to cook on and tables to eat on will for no reason carry their food for a mile at night and cook it on a rock and then sit on the ground in a circle and sing?" His voice was heavy with sarcasm.

"Well," I admitted, "seen through your eyes, I can believe that my explanation sounds pretty stupid. But, really, there was nothing more to it than I've said. Perhaps it's a streak of madness in Americans that makes us like to do it, but it has nothing to do with worship of the rain god." I was never sure whether they finally accepted our innocence or if they still suspected us of being secret idolaters.

How Far Can I Go?

Paul tells the Corinthians, in essence, "You are asking the wrong questions. You are asking, 'Is it permissible?' when you ought to be asking, 'Is it beneficial?' and 'Is it constructive?' "

The apostle warned them to not carry the issue of

meat offered to idols too far. If there was no question of jeopardizing their influence, or injuring their own conscience, eat it. He was referring to meat offered at pagan temples but subsequently sold to the city butcher. "Eat anything sold in the meat market without raising questions of conscience, for, 'The earth is the Lord's, and everything in it.' If some unbeliever invites you to a meal and you want to go, eat whatever is put before you without raising questions of conscience. But if anyone says to you, 'This has been offered in sacrifice,' then do not eat it, both for the sake of the man who told you and for conscience' sake—the other man's conscience, I mean, not yours" (1 Corinthians 10:25-29).

"You are asking, 'Is it permissible?' when you ought to be asking, 'Is it beneficial?' and 'Is it constructive?' "

The "anyone" raising the objection is not likely the host, since if he had suspected the meat would be objectionable to his Christian guests, he would either not have served it or would not have invited Christians in the first place. It was probably another Christian guest who had a conscience problem with eating the meat or else a heathen who knew just enough about the Christian religion to know that its followers avoided sacrifices made to the pagan gods. Paul is saying that the invited Christian guest should not create a problem by asking the host: "Was this meat offered at some temple?" On the other hand, if someone else brings it up, the Christian should not ignore that a problem has arisen. Obviously, the objector feels that the Christian should not eat the meat. If he goes ahead and eats it anyway, that person is going to be offended, and the

Christian loses credibility with him.

There are some Christians who regard the restriction against eating blood and strangled animals (Acts 15:20) as having a continuous application. A great many others believe it was given only on a basis of influence in order to ease the confrontation between Jewish and Gentile churches. They have no problem with eating blood sausage and chickens and rabbits which have not been bled. It would be callous and offensive for a Christian who has no conscience problem with eating food containing blood to try to impose it upon another Christian who regards it as sin.

The principle of avoiding being offensive is also applicable when a Christian invites a non-Christian to a meal. It would be shameful to serve a Muslim guest pork or a Hindu guest beef.

Demon Tables Today

We could say that we no longer have the Corinthian problem of eating at a demon's table, but we would be wrong. Just as the Corinthians denied the existence of the pagan gods yet gave them life by allowing them to infest their lives, so we live in a world of demons that are waiting at the door to be allowed inside our hearts. To delight in evil demons such as alcohol, drugs, illicit sex, and violence, we allow Satan to impair our relationship with Christ just as the heathen idols did.

One demon who will seize every opportunity to occupy a chair at our table is the god Mammon—the demon of *materialism* who will make us the slave of physical things. It is so difficult not to be owned by our possessions, to resist the smiling, fat-jowled god with the greedy eyes. He promises so much and yet always pulls the pot of gold just out of our reach after spilling a few coins, so that we are forever reaching for what we don't yet have. We pay lip service to the self-discipline which Paul defines in 1 Timothy 6:8: "If we have food and clothing, we will be content with that." But our hearts continue to want to build bigger barns and fill them to the rafters. We start out with the goal of providing a living for ourselves and our families, but materialism keeps on moving the goalposts. Like the Spanish explorer, Coronado, we wear ourselves out seeking the golden city of Cibola which is always just over the horizon. Seeking security is a natural impulse of humanity. But sometimes the search becomes so all-demanding that eternal things are neglected, and what was a God-given instinct to provide becomes a demon. And the most persistent demons are good intentions taken to excess.

> *The most persistent demons are good intentions taken to excess.*

Another demon that is a close companion of materialism is *anxiety*. It eats like a corrosive acid into the tranquility and confidence of our hearts. Paul urged "Do not be anxious about anything, but in everything, by prayer and petition, with thanksgiving, present your requests to God" (Philippians 4:6). Yet he was human and he worried, for he says in 2 Corinthians 11:28: "Besides everything else, I face daily the pressure of my concern for all the churches." The word "concern" (Greek, *merimna*) is exactly the same word Jesus used for "anxieties of life" that he warned us to be careful of in Luke 21:34. Feeling deep concern for problems, both our own and of others, is again a God-given emotion that motivates us to solve the problems we are able to handle.

But when anxiety erodes our faith in God's providence and robs us of quiet trust that all things will work for the good of those who love him (Romans 8:28), it has become a destructive demon.

A common demon who resides wherever he can is the demon of *expediency* and *situation ethics.* We live in a society where things are rarely what they claim to be. One cynic remarked, "If you want the small size of anything you must ask for the "large"; medium size is "extra large" and large is "giant size." A Russian visitor to the states was explaining to a friend: "When an American says to you, 'we must have lunch together sometime,' what he really means is he never intends to have lunch with you. If he really does, he'll set the time and place." People who are scrupulously honest often find it very difficult to hold a job in the business world. Secretaries are expected, even required, to tell a caller the boss is not in when he is. Used car salesmen are expected to present an often-owned model as having only been owned by an elderly lady who treated it like her own child.

In a slave market in the Old South, an affluent planter approached a teenage boy who was up for sale. He was the son of Christian slave parents but, as was common in those unfortunate times, he was separated from his family and put on the auction block. "Boy," the well-groomed man addressed him, "if I buy you, will you be honest?" The young man replied, "I'll be honest whether you buy me or not." His body was for sale but not his conscience.

The colorful pioneer preacher, "Raccoon" John Smith, made the decision to abandon denominationalism and devote his energies to the Restoration movement of getting back to the church of the Bible. He was warned that he would lose his income and in all probability lose his farm. He replied, "I have never yet offered my conscience for sale in the marketplace, but if I should ever decide to do so, it would take more than that sixty-acre farm to buy it."

Satan uses the particular demon who is most likely to compromise our allegiance to Christ.

Satan uses the particular demon who is most likely to compromise our allegiance to Christ. Many fall prey to the demon of *bitterness*, holding on to old grievances until they erode their relationships to people and to God. The writer of Hebrews warned: "See to it that no one misses the grace of God and that no bitter root grows up to cause trouble and defile many" (12:15). The names of Gilbert and Sullivan will be linked as long as the world stands for the brilliant operettas which that talented pair produced. In real life they harbored a grudge to the degree that they would not speak to each other and only communicated in writing.

If we give these demons a place in our hearts, if we "delight in evil," they are like the eggs that the cuckoo lays in the nest of another bird. They grow until they have ousted the rightful occupant of our hearts and eventually destroy our communion with the Lord. "You cannot have a part in both the Lord's table and the table of demons."

Answering God's Call

God's call to salvation in Jesus Christ is not only a call to a new relationship but is also a call to a changed lifestyle. A Christian's life must coincide with his message. When we profess one thing but exemplify another in our behavior, we cause the gospel to be rejected and blasphemed. Paul told the

Corinthians that they were like a letter "known and read by everybody" (2 Corinthians 3:2). It is the "Christ in us" that is the message the world will get (Colossians 1:27). Christianity in general is not particularly attractive to the secular world because non-Christians do not see the commitment to the principles the church espouses in the lives of those who call themselves Christians.

This inconsistency between the lives and the message of Christians is perhaps Satan's most effective tool in keeping the unbeliever separated from God, and Satan spends great energy in exploiting it. When unbelievers see Christians delighting in evil rather than in the love of Christ, they lose respect for these hypocrites. A Christian never "sits down or walks along the road" (Deuteronomy 6:7) that the devil doesn't at least try to provide a demon as his companion.

Whatever we do in interfacing with the unsaved world, we have to consider carefully whether we are sharing the table of life with Christ or with demons (1 Corinthians 10:21).

Focusing Your Faith

1. What activities or events do some people consider "pagan rituals" that others would see as permissible or even as opportunities to glorify Christ?

2. How do you feel when someone decides for you what you can or can't do according to Scripture?

3. Have you ever attended a company party or special event in which you felt uncomfortable and didn't know whether to participate or risk rudeness and leave? What did you choose to do?

4. What demon do you invite to dinner most regularly? (Anxiety? Materialism? Bitterness, etc.?)

5. How can we escape from the demons' grasp once they have us? Who would you ask to help you?

6. Think of a time when you had to forego an activity because of the conscience of a "weaker brother." How did you feel about that?

7. Have you ever been the "weaker brother" who placed limitations on someone else? How do you feel about that now?

1 Corinthians 11:20-22

When you come together, it is not the Lord's Supper you eat, for as you eat, each of you goes ahead without waiting for anybody else. One remains hungry, another gets drunk. Don't you have homes to eat and drink in? Or do you despise the church of God and humiliate those who have nothing? What shall I say to you? Shall I praise you for this? Certainly not!

Chapter 9

Communion

Confusion

1 Corinthians 10:14-17;
11:17-34

One of the stories in *The Arabian Nights* concerns a poor beggar on the city streets who was invited to dinner by Barmecide, a wealthy, Persian nobleman. When they were seated

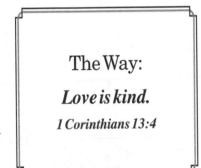

The Way:

Love is kind.

1 Corinthians 13:4

for the meal, Barmecide passed the man one choice "dish" after another, even though the man could see nothing but empty air. Barmecide exclaimed over the tastiness of each course and pressed his poor guest to eat more. Finally, the beggar could stand the charade no longer, and, springing to his feet, he angrily struck his host. Then Barmecide roared with laughter, and, after inviting the guest to be seated again, he clapped his hands and waiters brought in an actual feast. From this story, the expression "a

Barmecide's feast" has come to mean an occasion
that is empty of any real substance.

The Lord's Supper was intended by Christ to be a
deep spiritual experience for his followers. When we
eliminate the love represented by the Supper, we
reduce it to a binding duty that is little more than a
mechanical ritual. We make it into a "Barmecide's
feast" that neither honors our Lord nor provides any
real fellowship with either him or with our fellow
Christians.

Unity of the Body

The underlying theme of 1 Corinthians is the love
and unity of the body. The church at Corinth had
violated this unity by forming themselves into
parties, seeking occasions for lawsuits against one
another, vying for prominence in the assembly, and,
in general, lacking love for one another. But perhaps
nowhere was disunity more obvious than in the
Lord's Supper. They had strayed so far from the kind
spirit of communion that whatever group arrived
first at the designated meeting would not hesitate to
eat all the bread and drink all the wine. Even if their
commitment to Christ was too shallow for them to
relate the bread and the wine to the sacrifice made
for their sins, common human kindness toward their
fellow Christians should have prevented their eating
ahead of the others. "One remains hungry, another
gets drunk" (11:21).

Paul pleads with the Corinthian church: "I speak
to sensible people; judge for yourselves what I say. Is
not the cup of thanksgiving[1] for which we give
thanks a participation in the blood of Christ? And is
not the bread that we break a participation in the
body of Christ? Because there is one loaf, we, who
are many, are one body, for we all partake of the one

loaf" (1 Corinthians 10:15-17).

Old Testament Roots

Since it is virtually impossible to understand what was happening at the communion service in Corinth without understanding the Jewish Passover ritual, it will be helpful to look at the roots of the Lord's Supper in the Old Testament.

The Lord's Supper grew out of the general context of the Passover meal, or Seder, as it is called by Jews today. It was during this that Jesus instituted his memorial feast.

Passover was one of the most important institutions of Judaism. The regulations for observing it are found in Exodus 12. It was to be kept on the evening of the fourteenth day of the first Hebrew month (Abib or Nisan). Preparation began on the tenth day of the month when the lamb for the Passover sacrifice was put up in preparation for the feast. The lamb (or kid) was killed at the evening on the fourteenth, one lamb for each family, or two small families could share.

The blood was put on the sides and top of the door frame of the house where the lamb was to be eaten. The lamb was roasted whole and eaten with unleavened bread and bitter herbs. Any of the lamb left after the meal was burned before morning. The people themselves were to be dressed, ready for travel with their belts buckled, sandals on their feet, and walking sticks in their hands. It is also understood that they were standing.

Passover could be upon any day of the week. It was followed by the seven days of unleavened bread with holy convocations (or special Sabbaths) on the fifteenth and twenty-first days of Nisan. This explains why the Sabbath following Jesus' crucifixion is called a *high day* ("day of Preparation," John 19:31). It was not necessarily a weekly Sabbath.

When we come to the Jewish celebration of Passover in New Testament times, we find some changes have taken place. The Jews no longer are eating it dressed as for a journey. They recline on couches with their shoes off. They have added salad dressing for the bitter herbs (*charoseth* or sop) and they are making sandwiches. But a more significant change is the addition of the cup of wine, nowhere mentioned in the Old Testament. They, in fact, have four cups of wine during the course of the Passover ritual, and they called the third cup the *kos habberakah*, or "cup of blessing." Why it was called that they didn't know. Paul implies in 1 Corinthians 10:16 that it was the cup blessed at the Lord's Supper.

A Day Early?

It has been argued that Jesus and his disciples took Passover a day early, on the thirteenth day of Nisan. This is *not possible* for the following reasons:

1. The gospels clearly establish that it was the correct day. Matthew states (26:17), "Now the first day of unleavened bread the disciples came to Jesus saying, 'Where do you want us to make preparation for you to eat the Passover?'"

Mark says (14:12), "On the first day of the Feast of Unleavened Bread, when it was customary to sacrifice the Passover lamb, Jesus' disciples asked him, 'Where do you want us to go and make preparations for you to eat the Passover?'"

Luke is even more definite (22:7), "Then came the day of Unleavened Bread on which the Passover lamb had to be sacrificed."

2. Passover itself was a symbol of the death of

Jesus (1 Corinthians 5:7). It would be inappropriate if Jesus himself had been sacrificed on another day.

3. The room where Jesus and his disciples met was prepared already for the feast. There was nothing miraculous or even unusual about that, since Jewish custom required residents of Jerusalem to make prepared rooms available for out-of-town visitors. They provided everything, including a basin of water and a towel, except the actual food. The miraculous element was Jesus' prediction that they would meet a man carrying a pitcher of water.

The reason some have thought that Jesus and his disciples kept the feast a day early is that on the morning of Jesus' trial the priests and Pharisees refused to enter the palace "to avoid ceremonial uncleanness," and "be able to eat the Passover" (John 18:28). This is a misunderstanding of the circumstances. Ceremonial uncleanness of this type could never prevent a Jew's eating the Passover lamb because of the provision of Leviticus 11 that he could wash at evening and be clean. The ceremonial meal they would have been excluded from was not Passover supper, but the *Chagigah*, or festive meal, which took place on the afternoon of the fourteenth.

Conflicts Concerning Communion

Some other problems have been encountered in the accounts of the institution of the Lord's Supper as recorded in the gospels:

1. How many cups? Fortunately, the Passover *haggadah*[2] helps us here. It states, "Let each have his own cup or glass." Jewish practice has always required a cup for each celebrant which was filled four times during the evening. Luke's account also helps to clear up the matter. Luke 22:17 says that

Jesus took the cup and told his disciples, "Take this and divide it among you." Since verse 20 makes it clear that they did not drink the cup until after the bread was eaten, it is a necessary inference that they had something to divide the wine into. In fact, a correct translation of the Greek text of verse 20 clears up the matter: "This cup which has been poured out for you is the New Testament in my blood."

The language shows conclusively that it was the *cup* which had been poured out, not Jesus' blood which had been shed. (This is because a Greek adjectival participle must agree with the noun it modifies in gender, number, and case. "Having been poured out" agrees with cup, but not with blood.) This is not the case, however, in Matthew 26:28 and Mark 14:24, where the reference is to blood specifically. This is not intended to imply that it is wrong for a congregation to use a single cup. The symbolism is in the contents of the cup or cups. The container is irrelevant.

2. Should wine or grape juice be used? The expression *fruit of the vine* used in the synoptic gospels (Matthew, Mark, and Luke) means "the product of the vine." This applies equally to grape juice or fermented wine. It comes from the Hebrew *peri hagephen*, which is literally "fruit of the vine," but most generally referred to what we call wine. However, the Hebrews usually used the general word *yayin* (wine) to include the grape juice from the time it was squeezed out into the wine vat through the whole fermentation process until it finally became vinegar.

The grape harvest in Israel comes in September. Passover occurs in late March or early April. Since pasteurization was still eighteen centuries away from Jesus' time, they could not preserve grape juice. It fermented quickly into wine. The Talmud restricted saying the *kiddush* (blessing) to red wine by forbidding "white wine, black wine, raisin wine, cellar wine, and wine on the lees." I have a letter from Professor Rabinowitz, former chief rabbi of Jerusalem, which states that Jews have never used anything other than the ordinary red wine of Palestine, mixed with three parts water, for Passover. The Talmud, indeed, forbade saying the blessing over the wine until after the water was added. The practice was so constant, even for ordinary use, that the word for pouring wine in Hebrew, *mazag*, really means mix.

Some have argued that the Jews cooked grape juice down into grape syrup and preserved it that way, and at Passover they reconstituted it to grape juice by adding water. I inquired into this alleged practice while visiting in Jerusalem and was assured by the Jews there that they do not practice nor have ever practiced this. This argument seems to be more apologetic than historical or exegetical.

It is historically probable that Jesus used ordinary red wine to inaugurate the Lord's Supper. Some have adopted the view that since Jesus used it we are bound to do the same. Their argument looks plausible on the surface, but let's look further:

- The gospels do not specify unleavened bread. We use it because we know Jesus used it at Passover. (We cannot, however, prove conclusively that it is wrong to use leavened bread.)

- The gospels do not specify wine, but since the Jews always used wine at Passover, and therefore Jesus would have used it, we are bound to use fermented wine.

These are not true parallels. In the first place, the Law of Moses *required* unleavened bread, whereas there is no instruction whatever in the Law regarding the cup.

Second, it was practically possible to have leavened or unleavened bread at any time. Therefore, their use of unleavened bread was based upon a principle, not on practical expediency. The use of wine was a practical expedient because grape juice was unobtainable. In congregations where a problem arises over which to use, it might be expedient to provide both rather than have division in the body.

Those who must, as a matter of conscience, use fermented wine for the Lord's Supper, should mix it with three parts water to be consistent with Jewish practice.

3. *Did Luke reverse the order of blessing the bread and wine?* Luke 22:17 (KJV) reads, "And he took the cup, and gave thanks. . . ." Verse 19 says, "And he took bread, and gave thanks. . . ." The translation is at fault here and has given rise to this misunderstanding. "Having given thanks" is referring to the thanksgiving which closed the Passover meal itself, as the Passover *haggadah* shows clearly. The fellowship meal following Passover was introduced with the third cup, the cup of blessing. After Jesus had given thanks for the Passover meal, he took the third cup and told his disciples to divide it among themselves, which they did. He then offered thanks for the loaf, broke it and gave to them. Verse 20 translates, "Also the cup, in the same way, after eating, saying. . . ." The order of events was (1) Jesus closed the Passover meal with the offering of thanks, (2) he took the cup of wine and told his disciples to divide it among themselves, (3) he took the loaf, offered thanks, broke it, and gave it to them, and

(4) after they had eaten, he took the cup, the contents of which already had been poured into their cups, gave thanks for it, and the disciples (but not Jesus) drank the wine.

Changes in the Supper

The fellowship meal (called *chabburah* in Hebrew, *aphikomen* in Greek) included the drinking of the third cup and the eating of the half of the loaf left from Passover. One of the Hallel psalms was then sung, and the meal was concluded with the drinking of the fourth cup. This fellowship meal was kept by early Christians in connection with the Lord's Supper and was called the *agape*, or "love feast." It is mentioned in the New Testament only in Jude 12 but is under discussion in 1 Corinthians 11:17-22 because the Corinthians had allowed it to overshadow and virtually displace the Lord's Supper. This abuse led first to a separation between the Lord's Supper and the agape, and still later to the disappearance of the latter.

The Corinthians were partaking of the Lord's Supper "unworthily" because they were not "discerning" (remembering in their hearts) the body and blood which it symbolized. This has led some, conscious of their shortcomings, to feel unworthy to partake of the Supper. It is precisely because we are unworthy of God's grace that we need a crucified Savior, which is what we are publicly professing or "showing forth" in partaking of the Lord's Supper. We must take great care, however, that we do not partake of it casually or frivolously; otherwise, we are showing dishonor to the symbols of Christ's death on the cross.

Very early in the second century the concept of the Lord's Supper as a symbolic commemorative communion was changed into a saving sacrament. One popular Christian writer of the first quarter of that century went so far as to call it "the medicine of salvation." Soon after, it was proposed that only an ordained bishop could administer communion since it consisted of holy elements that no unconsecrated hand must touch.

It was inevitable that such sacramentalism would lead to the bread and wine's being identified as the literal flesh and blood of Christ. The view that the bread and wine become the actual and physical body and blood of Christ derives from Augustine's interpretation of John 6:53-56. Later in life, after more thorough study, Augustine reversed himself and said that the context is belief in Jesus as our perfect sacrifice, not the taking of the Lord's Supper. The context is set in verse 47 where Jesus says, "He who believes has eternal life. I am the bread of life." He concludes his talk on the living bread by saying that the one eating his flesh and drinking his blood is the one who dwells in him and he in that person. The one who lives in Jesus by faith constantly partakes of that atoning sacrifice, and "the blood of Jesus, [God's] Son, purifies us from all sin" (1 John 1:7). The elements of the Lord's Supper are bread and wine and are not altered substantially or sacramentally by the blessing. They are the Lord's Supper only in the heart of the true believer who is remembering the body and blood of the Lord.

Purposes of the Lord's Supper

According to the New Testament, the Lord's Supper has three purposes:

1. It is a memorial of Jesus' broken body and shed blood (1 Corinthians 11:24; see also Luke 22:19).

2. It is a profession of our faith (a "showing forth") in Jesus' death and in his second coming (1 Corinthians 11:26).

3. It is a self-evaluation of our continuing relationship with Christ—a "quality check" of our spiritual integrity and fervency (1 Corinthians 11:27-30).

4. It exemplifies the love and unity of all Christians (1 Corinthians 10:17).

The Corinthian church had violated all four of these purposes. They were so intent upon satisfying their appetites that it was impossible for them to reverence the memory of Christ's body and blood. Rather than demonstrating their faith in Christ's death and second coming, they were showing greediness and selfishness. And instead of exemplifying the loving kindness and the unity of the church, they were institutionalizing the division that already existed in spirit. It is little wonder that the apostle exclaimed in disgust, "Your meetings do more harm than good" (11:17).

Many Christians have been intimidated by Paul's statement that whoever abuses the Lord's Supper "eats and drinks judgment on himself" (11:29). So, rather than risk taking it "unworthily" (11:27), they abstain altogether. As already stated, no Christian is "worthy" to partake of it. It is a privilege given to redeemed sinners who are confessing that our salvation is made possible only by Christ's broken body and shed blood. It is a eucharist (thanksgiving) for God's grace in saving us.

Some religious groups have taken upon themselves to monitor who is worthy and who is unworthy to partake of communion upon the premise that allowing a heretic or unbeliever to commune would not only be profaning the Lord's Supper itself but

would be allowing the unworthy person to eat and
drink damnation to his soul. That is dangerously
sacramental. There is no magic for good or bad in
the bread and grape juice. The communion between
the heart of the believer and his Lord is spiritual,
and the physical elements only symbolize the spiritual realities. We don't need to worry about the
wrong person participating. The table is the Lord's
(10:21) and is in his kingdom. So no one who was not
in communion with him has ever truly taken the
Lord's Supper. In the words of the Restoration
fathers: "We neither invite nor debar." As Paul said
to the Corinthians who had vulgarized the occasion
of communion: "When you come together, it is not
the Lord's Supper you eat" (11:20).

"Unless you change your heart you probably never will actually take the Lord's Supper."

What we need to be serious and prayerful about
when we take communion is that we do indeed eat
the Lord's Supper and not simply participate in a
habitual, perfunctory, and, therefore, meaningless
ritual that we call the Lord's Supper. There are
those who show up to take the loaf and the cup
thinking they have satisfied all they really have to
do for the week to maintain their relationship to
Christ. But when it is taken as simply satisfying a
legal requirement, it has no meaning and is, in fact,
an insult to the Lord.

A question that should never be asked is, "Do I
have to take communion every Sunday?" because the
obvious answer is, "Unless you change your heart
you probably never will actually take the Lord's
Supper." As a gracious privilege and act of love, it is
a great blessing. As a burdensome and resented

obligation, it is an affront to our Savior just as the blemished offerings the Israelites made to God were (Malachi 1:6-14).

Common Questions

Nearly any discussion of the Lord's Supper raises questions. Some of those most commonly asked are the following:

1. Is there a command to break bread every first day of the week? Not as such. Jesus instructed Christians: "Do this in remembrance of me" (1 Corinthians 11:24). Whether you regard it as a command to be obeyed or a glorious privilege to be joyfully embraced will depend upon your orientation. We understand from Acts 20:7 that the first Christians were accustomed to breaking bread on the first day of the week, and from 1 Corinthians 16:2 that they met every first day. By the early second century some were practicing it at special meetings on other days as well. Whether the first century churches ever took communion on any other day than the first is not known. Some believe that they did, based upon Paul's expression, "Whenever you eat this bread and drink this cup" (1 Corinthians 11:26), but that is not at all conclusive.

2. Is it permissible to take the Supper more than once on a Sunday? Some itinerant evangelists, and especially missionaries, often meet with several gatherings of Christians every Sunday. What should they do: Take communion with each group to show the unity and fellowship of believers, or explain that they have already taken it? Individuals are going to give different answers because it is, after all, a decision that no individual or group can impose upon someone else.

3. How does our manner of taking communion differ from first-century practice? Since the Lord's Supper originated on the occasion of Passover, it is likely that the first group of Jewish Christians (house churches) followed largely the format of the Passover fellowship meal. That is, they reclined on couches at a long, low table (or tables) and partook of an actual meal of bread and wine, not simply a token taste of each as we do today.

The custom of many twentieth-century congregations of having the servers of the communion meet in a side room or at the back and then march out to take their places in front of the congregation did not come from the New Testament era. It arose from Constantine's "parade of the clergy" in fourth century Byzantine churches. Its purpose was to establish the dignity of the clergy above the ordinary members, the laity.

The tendency to have communion tables of a boxlike design placed in front of the pulpit derives from the old Roman law courts where the sacrificial altar was placed in front of the magistrate's throne. The two side chairs were for the magistrate's two assessors, or advisers. The lectern itself was not placed in front of the center chair on the pulpit for more than one thousand years. Early teachers (preachers) spoke from the center chair while seated (*ex cathedra*, from the chair).

These details are inconsequential, of course, as they only reflect changing customs and convenience. As soon as churches were able to build their own meeting places (from the third century on), it is certain that the practice of reclining at table for the communion was abandoned for a more orderly and efficient system of serving the bread and the wine, since the Passover model was only practical for small groups in house churches.

4. *Would it be scriptural for women to pass the communion?* It is neither scriptural nor unscriptural, but nonscriptural, since we have no New Testament model on which to base our practice. Problems with doing it are probably based upon the tradition of a leadership role in serving communion dating from Constantine's time. It can be argued that it is a serving role, not a leadership role, entirely consistent with using either male or female servants.

5. *Did early Christians take communion on Saturday night or Sunday?* It is likely (from Acts 20:7) that the first Christians took it on Saturday night. Since the major part of the church was at first Jewish, and the first day of the week began for them at dusk on Saturday evening, it is logical to conclude that they would have met then. This is made more likely by two other factors: (1) Since many (or most) Christians were either slaves or else belonged to the working class, they would have found it difficult to meet during daylight hours, and (2) it would have accorded well with their families' practice of taking Passover between dusk and midnight.

We know from a letter written to the Emperor Trajan about A.D. 115 by Pliny, governor of Bithynia, that Christians by that time had changed the time to "before dawn on Sunday morning." That suggests that the growing proportion of Gentiles in the church were not comfortable with breaking bread on Saturday night since they followed Roman time (midnight to midnight).

Circumstances forced them to meet during hours of darkness. Since Jewish Christians could not observe the Lord's Supper on Sunday night (it was already Monday by their time) they had worked out

a compromise to accompany both viewpoints by
meeting at a time both could agree was the first day
of the week. Time is, in any case, relative. Christians
on one side of the international date line may take
communion on what to them is Sunday, whereas
Christians on the other side but only ten miles away
may take it twenty-four hours earlier.

6. *If it is impossible to meet with other saints for
communion due to illness or other unavoidable
circumstances, is it permissible to break bread alone?*
Again, this is a nonscriptural question, since there is
no New Testament answer. Whether a Christian
does or does not practice it will depend upon his view
of what constitutes the *principal* purpose of communion: (1) affirming the unity of the church by
many "breaking one loaf," or (2) remembering the
Lord's death. It will also be partially determined by
one's definition of fellowship—whether physical
closeness or spiritual unity. One may feel that he is
partaking only with those who are convened with
him in the same room. Another may affirm that she
is fellowshipping and affirming the unity of all
Christians everywhere, even though they may be
separated by many time zones. The only reasonable
solution to the question is individual conscience
(Romans 14:4-6).

In spite of differing viewpoints on some aspects of
the Lord's Supper, there is no occasion for a spirit of
division to arise over them as long as we are willing
to show love and kindness, tolerate each other's
weaknesses, and strive for unity. The memorial love
feast is perhaps in itself the most unifying element in
the Christian experience—not only between believer
and believer, but between believers and their Lord.
We should never let matters of expediency become

"roots of bitterness" among us because "Love is kind."

<hr>

Notes:

[1] The NIV incorrectly translates *eulogia* (blessing) as "thanksgiving" in 10:16. Paul's expression "the cup of blessing" (literally, the cup of the blessing) is the exact equivalent of the Hebrew *kos habberakah* for the third cup of Passover. Thanks was certainly expressed for the cup (Matthew 26:27; Mark 14:23) and for the bread (Luke 22:19; 1 Corinthians 11:24), but the expression in 1 Corinthians 10:16 is "the cup of [the] blessing."

[2] The Passover *haggadah* is the Jewish order of the ritual Passover.

Focusing Your Faith

1. What is Thanksgiving dinner in your family like?
    What is most meaningful to you about it?

2. Describe the most meaningful communion ser-
    vice you've ever experienced.

3. After studying the history of the Lord's Supper,
    how would you evaluate your congregation's
    "rules" concerning communion?

4. What song best expresses your feelings about
    communion with your Lord and your church?

5. What role does the Lord's Supper play in the job
    of evangelism (11:26)? What would a visitor who
    knew nothing about Christ learn from observing
    your communion service?

6. How would you feel if you were a visitor in a
    church that had decided to follow the early
    church's example of combining a meal with
    communion?

7. Have you ever declined communion because you
    didn't feel your life was right? How could com-
    munion help that situation?

1 Corinthians 14:33-35

For God is not a God of disorder but of peace.

As in all congregations of the saints, women should remain silent in the churches. They are not allowed to speak, but must be in submission, as the Law says. If they want to inquire about something, they should ask their own husbands at home; for it is disgraceful for a woman to speak in the church.

Chapter 10

What About Women?

1 Corinthians 11:2-16;
14:33-35

A half century ago I was involved in establishing a congregation among the Gwembi people of the remote Zambezi valley. About forty people were baptized, about evenly

> ## The Way:
>
> *Love perseveres.*
>
> 1 Corinthians 13:7

divided between men and women. Because of the distance and the fact that travel was on foot, two years were to elapse before we again visited that little church. We arrived at midday on a Sunday and found the service already in progress—attended by twenty women and only one man. The situation was not unique; it had happened many times in many places.

If Jesus' promise that the gates of Hades will not prevail against his church is to be fulfilled (and if that is not taking the scripture out of context) then it

will be the godly women who love him who will
ensure its fulfillment. The church is alive in many
places throughout the world because of the love of
women disciples who persevered because of their
love for Christ.

As women eagerly search for ways to serve Christ
using their God-given gifts and talents, the question
often arises, What about women? What role should
women have in the church? More and more women
are becoming dissatisfied with the passive role of
"pewpacker." For some it's a difficult switch to make
from corporate manager on Friday to church ob-
server on Sunday. They want to participate in the
growth of the church family they love so intensely,
and yet they are often prevented from serving in the
way they are gifted. A fresh examination of the
Scriptures will help settle the dilemma.

Restoration Restrictions

Restoration churches have generally severely
restricted the public role of women in the ministries
of the congregations on the premise that the New
Testament forbids any public function of women.
Such passages as Acts 21:9 and Philippians 4:2, 3
indicate that women probably filled a more active
place in the public ministry of the Word in the first
century than they have in the last 1200 years. We
certainly do not want our women (or men, for that
matter) violating clear New Testament instruction.
On the other hand, we do not want the church
functioning at half-capacity through applying traditional interpretations of Scripture that the text itself
does not justify. In other words, keeping the train on
the right track is not best served by swerving too far
to the right in order to keep the train from derailing
on the left.

For example, most Restoration churches would be very uncomfortable with women passing the elements of communion even though serving food and drink is normally regarded as a service function rather than a leadership function. This prejudice is tradition-based rather than Bible-based, due to the concept which developed early in church history that "administering communion" was a priestly office restricted to the clergy only. Possibly the fact that the servers of communion stand while the congregation is seated may contribute to our misgivings.

> *We do not want the church functioning
> at half-capacity through applying
> traditional interpretations of Scripture
> that the text itself does not justify.*

That factor may also explain why we have no women song leaders (even though no reference to song leaders appears in the New Testament). In spite of the fact that the soprano is the leading part in most of our hymns (and there are few male sopranos) we prefer having a male leading the song an octave low to having a woman start it, possibly because the song leader usually stands before the congregation. In some churches in third world countries, a woman often begins the song in accordance with their normal cultural practice. No male feels that his "authority" is being flouted because starting a song is not regarded as any assertion of power or dominance over anyone else.

The person we call the preacher or pulpit minister, that is, the public teacher of the congregation, was the *prophet* of New Testament times. He corresponded to the messenger of the congregation (*sheliach tsibbur*) in the Jewish synagogue. Can

women be public teachers of the Word? Most would
say it depends on the situation.

***Perception is important in addressing the
question of what is the permissible role of
women in the public teaching of the Word.***

Perception is important in addressing the question of what is the permissible role of women in the
public teaching of the Word. A curious application of
this occurred among the villagers of Zambia. I used
to make evangelistic trips during the dry season,
traveling by foot from village to village with porters
carrying my camping gear. At night in the village
two fires would be built a short distance apart. At
one the men and boys would cluster and at the other
the women and girls. Protocol demanded that I
stand at the men's fire and address them. The
women were unofficial listeners. Sister Myrtle Rowe
would teach in the same villages but at different
times. Then the roles were reversed! She would
stand at the women's fire and preach to them with
the men listening in from their campfire. In this way
a female teacher could function as effectively as a
male preacher and at the same time cultural impera-
tives were satisfied.

When I was a youth, the minister at our local
congregation taught the ladies' Bible class. When it
came time for the prayer (led by a woman) the
minister would step around the corner into the "cry
room" and listen in over the speaker. Thus his
"authority" was not violated!

Women as Leaders

In the early church women played an important
role. Let's look closely at some of the verses that

discuss their position.

As we approach the question of whether 1 Corinthians 14:34, 35 forbids women addressing or teaching an audience in which men are present, some general observations may be made:

1. In both Old and New Testament periods there is a clear and overwhelming priority of male leadership. From Paul's supporting arguments in 1 Corinthians 11:3, 7-10; 14:35; and 1 Timothy 2:13-15, it seems clear that male leadership is not subject to flexible guidelines but is a fixed order from the creation. In other words, male leadership is certainly the norm or general rule, not only in Bible history but in virtually all cultures.

God nevertheless not only sanctioned but implemented female leadership when it was needed. Even though such examples as Deborah, Hulda, and Anna were rare exceptions, they serve to illustrate that female leadership in working out God's purposes is legitimate in some circumstances. And since Paul's arguments are based upon a fundamental and everlasting order of submission, the same exceptions would apply in any age.

2. It is apparent, therefore, that the overriding consideration is the accomplishing of God's work, not the sex of the agent who performs it.

3. Female leadership promoted purely to establish equality of the sexes is not a legitimate reason for ignoring the priority of the norm, which is male leadership.

Women as Prophets

The word _prophetes_ (prophet) is not exclusive to the Bible. It was in common use throughout the Mediterranean world. It meant "an interpreter of the gods; one who speaks for a god; one with oracular power; an interpreter or expounder of the will of a god." In the biblical context, it meant a special spokesperson who proclaimed, declared, or expounded the will of God to people, generally by inspiration (although not always, as 1 Corinthians 14:30 shows clearly). After the New Testament period, *prophet* was used to designate a preacher or evangelist, as shown by the *Didache*[1], written about A.D. 115.

> *There is no period of biblical history*
> *in which the prophetic office was*
> *not shared by women.*

There is no period of biblical history in which the prophetic office was not shared by women.

• During the wilderness wanderings, Miriam was a prophetess (Exodus 15:20; Numbers 12:2) and as such was also a leader of the people (Micah 6:4).

• During the period of the judges, Deborah was a prophetess (Judges 4:4) and also was the leader of the nation (Judges 4:5).

• During the period of the kingdom, Huldah gave instructions to the king, high priest, and other leaders of Judah (2 Kings 22:14-20).

• During the Exile, both the prophets and prophetesses among the Babylonian exiles were hampering Ezekiel's work. The point is not whether they were good or bad prophets or prophetesses, but that prophetesses were accepted as a matter of course by the Israelites (Ezekiel 13:17).

• During the reconstruction of Jerusalem, among the prophets who opposed Nehemiah's reforms was a prophetess named Noadiah, who appears to have been the leader (Nehemiah 6:14).

• In intertestamental Judaism, the period of time between the Old and New Testaments, Anna was a prophetess who actually lived in the temple in Jerusalem. According to Luke 2:38, "she gave thanks to God and spoke of [Jesus] to all those who were looking forward to the redemption in Jerusalem." Quite clearly Anna was preaching to both men and women. Since Jesus' parents had brought him to the temple to "present him to the Lord," they were inside the inner court (otherwise called "The Court of Women" or "The Treasury"). It was the only place in the sacred precincts where all Jews, men and women (but no Gentiles), could assemble. It was here that Jesus later preached (John 8:20).

• Prophetesses seem to have been taken as the norm in the early church (Acts 21:9; 1 Corinthians 11:4, 5).

Women or Wives?

There has been much discussion of whether women in 1 Corinthians 14:34 refers to women in general or wives. The persons referred to in this verse are *the women*, not *their women*. Their women would have been the normal way to refer to the wives of the prophets. The use of *women* with the article *the* is the usual Greek way to express the idea of women belonging to the same class as the males already referred to; therefore, "the women with the gift of prophecy." Verse 36, where Paul anticipates the Corinthian women's objection to being silenced on the basis of God's revelation requiring them to speak, bears out this conclusion. By the abruptness of Paul's question, it appears that the prophetesses argue that if they were forbidden to preach, the congregation would not receive the full message of

God. Paul replies by saying that there were prophets
who could give the full message, so it did not depend
upon the women speaking.

Women in Silence

In recent history there has been much discussion
about the silence of women in the church. There are
three words used in the New Testament to express
some degree of the idea of quietness, although they
are not synonyms. These words are *siopao, sigao,*
and *hesuchadzo.* Only *siopao* accurately expresses
the idea of "keeping silent."

1. *Siopao* (Matthew 26:63; Mark 3:4; 10:48; Acts
18:9) has the root meaning "to keep silent," although
the silence sometimes refers to only a specific thing,
such as keeping a secret. This word is not used in
either of the two passages (1 Corinthians 14:34 and
1 Timothy 2:11, 12) although many versions translate these passages as if *siopao* were used in the
original.

2. *Sigao* is the key word in 1 Corinthians 14:34. It
also is used in connection with the male prophets in
14:28, 30. Its root meaning is not "keep silent," but
"to get quiet or quiet down." Examples of its use are
found in Luke 20:26; Acts 12:17; 15:12, 13. It means
"to subside from clamor or disruptive speech." It is
used to this day by Greek teachers to quell a noisy
class of children.

3. *Hesuchadzo* (and its noun *hesuchia*) carries the
ideas of tranquility or peace. It does not carry the
idea of remaining completely silent at all. This can
be seen from its use in Acts 11:18, where Peter's
Jewish companions give up the argument but go on
speaking. A similar example is found in Acts 21:14.
This is very significant as this word is sometimes

translated "silence" or "keep silent" in 1 Timothy
2:11, 12.

Order in the Assembly

The problem Paul addresses in the Corinthian
assembly ("when the whole church comes together,"
14:23; "when you come together," v. 26) is that
confusion reigned in the public service to such a
degree that edification was impossible. The women's
speaking in the assembly was causing confusion
much like that of too many people speaking in
tongues (vv. 22-25).

Three points need to be made in connection with
the passage found in 1 Corinthians 14:33, 34. The
first is that his qualifying phrase, "As in all the
congregations of the saints," may conclude verse 33
and not introduce verse 34 (as the NASB does it). In
other words, God is not a God of disorder but of
order as in all congregations of the saints.

Secondly, "congregations" can be translated
"assemblies" and may be referring to all the assemblies of the Corinthian church rather than to all the
congregations throughout the world.

> *The Law nowhere forbids*
> *a woman to teach publicly.*

The third point is that Paul's appeal to the Law
("Women should remain silent in the churches. They
are not allowed to speak, but must be in submission,
as the Law says" v. 34) does not refer to speaking
specifically, but to a woman's being in submission.
The Law nowhere forbids a woman to teach publicly.

Since "God is not a God of disorder but of peace"
(14:33), Paul placed certain limits on all those who
would speak in the assemblies:

1. The tongue-speaking prophets are not to speak at all unless there is an interpreter.

2. Only two or three prophets may speak at the service.

3. If a prophet receives a message from the Spirit, the prophet currently preaching must get quiet and let the inspired messenger have the floor.

4. The prophetesses are not to interject and try to "take the floor."

5. Prophetesses are not to cross-question the speakers. (Note: The word used for *question* in verse 35 means "to question closely, to interrogate.")

If the prophetesses wanted to debate, they could take up the question with their *own men* (fathers, husbands, brothers) after they got home because it was disgraceful for them *to speak out*. The Greek word used here is *laleo* (to speak up or break the silence, to speak publicly). It corresponds closely to the English word *speak*, which may mean simply to say something, or may mean to be the speaker, depending on the context. For instance, we sometimes ask, "Who is the speaker today?" meaning, "Who is the person who is going to expound or preach?"

First Timothy is a letter giving instructions for regulating the Ephesian assembly: the reading and teaching of the Scriptures (1 Timothy 4:14); prayer (2:1-8); teaching or preaching (2:11, 12; 4:14); and other matters so the people may know how to behave themselves in "the church of the living God" (3:15).

In 1 Timothy 2:11, 12, the women are instructed to be peaceable and to not violate the prerogative of the designated teacher of the congregation. Apparently there was a problem in the Ephesian church with women (or a woman) disrupting the assembly.

Paul's instruction that women not teach must be considered in its context which in this case is in relation to the designated teacher. Women are not to "appoint themselves" (Greek, *authentein*) authority over the designated teacher. The word *hesuchadzo*, which is translated "silence" or "keep silent" in this passage, simply means "to behave peaceably" and has nothing to do with whether the woman can join in a discussion if invited to do so. In other words, Paul is saying that women have no right to violate the authority of the teacher. It would not be correct for us to prohibit a woman from teaching in all instances because of this verse; otherwise we would have to exclude women from being Bible school teachers, ladies class teachers, and even home Bible study teachers.

Women as Special Servants

The first example we have of women as special servants in a religious context is found in Exodus 38:8, where "the women who served at the entrance to the Tent of Meeting" (where the Israelites met for worship before the Tabernacle was built) contributed their bronze mirrors to make the laver. We find these special servants referred to again after the Tabernacle was built (1 Samuel 2:22). The nature of their service is not explained, only the fact that they served.

During the temple period, women were barred from the sacred enclosure and the priestly functions. But, then, so also were the men of eleven of the twelve tribes and even most of the tribe of Levi; only the descendants of Aaron could serve as priests.

We know so little of the specific rituals of the ancient synagogue that we cannot assert what role, if any, the women played. We do not know whether

men and women sat together in the oldest synagogues or even if women attended, but in the ruins
of ancient synagogues there is evidence that in large
synagogues (as in Alexandria) the women sat in a
balcony. But we may conclude from later practice
that the women certainly did not give the exhortation nor lead the assembly in prayer. On the other
hand, the ruins of ancient synagogues reveal that
they had rooms for housing and feeding strangers.
Therefore, it is likely that women not only looked
after the hospitality ministry of the synagogue but
also the orphaned children of the community (just as
they later did for the Christian church which was
based upon synagogue practice).

---

*It is likely that women not only looked
after the hospitality ministry of the
synagogue but also the orphaned children
of the community.*

It is probable, but not certain, that the traditional
role of women in the benevolence ministry of the
synagogue is reflected in Acts 6:1-6. In the Aramaic-
speaking synagogues in Jerusalem the women were
accustomed to distributing food to the needy, and
therefore, felt snubbed when they were not asked to
do so in the Jerusalem Christian community. The
word used in verse 1 is not the word *neglected*
(*aneleo* in Greek) but *paratheoreo*, which means
"ignore, take no notice of." The problem seems,
therefore, to be one not of neglecting starving widows, but of passing them by in not using them to do
what was their accustomed responsibility in the
synagogue. Therefore, seven deacons were appointed
to make sure that the Grecian widows and the
Hebrew widows had an equal opportunity to serve.

These men were not appointed to replace the women or take over their duties.

Dorcas (Acts 9:36-41) was almost certainly functioning as a deaconess in supervising the work of the "widows in need" (desolate widows) who were church-supported. It appears from the context that the "upper room" where she was placed was the sewing room of the congregation (and probably also the meeting place of a house church). The fact that she was not the benefactress of the widows, but rather was actively involved in their ministry, is indicated by the use of *meta* for "with" in verse 39 (a word that carries the significance of sharing a common interest).

The only New Testament passage applying the title *deaconess* is Romans 16:1, 2, but the reference shows that Phoebe was actively involved as a special servant of the Cenchrean church near Corinth. The fact that Paul uses the designation in such a matter-of-fact way indicates that deaconesses were accepted as the norm and not the exception.

Seven deacons were appointed to make sure that the Grecian widows and the Hebrew widows had an equal opportunity to serve.

The reference in 1 Timothy 3:11 ("In the same way, their wives are to be women worthy of respect, not malicious talkers but temperate and trustworthy in everything.") is to women of the same class as the deacons (therefore deaconesses). Here again *women* is used with the definite article *the* and without the qualifying pronoun, *their*. The argument that deacons' wives are referred to is linguistically unprovable. This passage is not listing qualifications of deacons' wives but deaconesses.

A careful examination of 1 Timothy 5:3-16 will
reveal that the "enrolled" (Greek, *catalogued*) widows dealt with in verses 9-15 are a different class of
widows who are distinct from the "widows in need"
of verses 3 and 5. The traditional confusion of this
distinction has forced impossible and incorrect
conclusions that the church cannot:

- Support a destitute widow who is only 59
  years old (v. 9);

- Help a widow who does not have a past
  history of diligent service and hospitality
  (v. 16);

- Support a widow who has not reared
  children (which would clearly contradict
  the provision of v. 4);

- Support a widow who had been married
  twice (v. 9).

If we accepted those incorrect conclusions, we would
have to conclude that young widows cannot receive
help from the church (if widows indeed is meant
here), and that if one of these poor widows should
ever remarry, she would be a reprobate from Christ.

We, in fact, know in the post-apostolic period that
these "enrolled widows" committed themselves to
certain responsibilities on behalf of the church such
as caring for the poor, the sick, and orphaned children that they could not reasonably abandon. Verse
12 implies that they have undertaken a sacred
obligation, a pledge to Christ, that is binding upon
them. Most probably, these enrolled widows were
deaconesses and the qualifications listed in verses 9
and 10 are applicable to widows who are being
considered for deaconess.

Disappearance of Deaconesses

The first reference to *deaconesses* in post-New Testament literature is in a letter written from Pliny, the governor of Bithynia, to the Emperor Trajan in A.D. 110 stating that he had arrested two deaconesses of the church there. Deaconesses were a regular part of church ministries during the first 500 years of the church in both the East and West. The *Catholic Encyclopedia* mentions that "in the time of Justinian [who died in A.D. 565] the deaconesses still held a position of importance."

> *Deaconesses were a regular part of church ministries during the first 500 years of the church in both the East and West.*

It was just this position of importance that led to the disappearance of deaconesses. In the early church, deacons and deaconesses were special ministers or servants of the congregation entrusted with specific functions rather than offices in the sense of importance and authority. After ordination became a mystical sacrament instead of a public recognition of special areas of responsibility, people began to have reservations about sacred ordination of women.

The Council of Orange (A.D. 441)[2] forbade appointment of deaconesses altogether, although in some areas they survived for several centuries (down to the eleventh century in the Greek church). Since the eighth-century Council of Vienna, the public function of females has been restricted in the Catholic church on the grounds that "a woman is too weak a vessel to bear the fire of ordination." From that time the office of the New Testament deaconess disappears. A woman's function as a public teacher

largely ceased as a result of the entrenchment of
"ordained clergy" over the "laity."

Early Bible translations contributed to the sub-
servient position of women to a degree not justified
by the original Greek text. The Reformation
churches inherited this perception from their Roman
Catholic roots and, like a host of other things, accepted this idea without critical re-appraisal because
more urgent issues commanded the attention of
their scholars. Since deaconesses were no longer in
the Catholic church at the time of the Reformation,
there was no immediate tradition for the reformers
to carry the institution into the Protestant movement. Restoration churches have generally not
seriously challenged these concepts. Consequently,
we have to go back into the ancient roots of the
church to show that deaconesses are no modern
innovation.

What Does the Bible Say?

What conclusions can we draw about God's plan
for women from this information?

1. God has in every age used women in the office
of prophecy as his public spokespersons just as he
has used men.

2. Inspired prophetesses were an integral part of
the New Testament church.

3. Under the prevailing disorderly conditions at
Corinth, Paul forbade women to be the public ex-
pounders of the Word or to lead the assembly in
prayer when the whole church was assembled in one
place.

4. Women are not to usurp the prerogative of the
designated teachers of the assembly.

5. A prophetess could lead public prayer or teach

publicly anywhere but in the assembled church; however, she must be careful not to leave the impression that she is no longer subject to her husband.

6. No restrictions are placed upon women's teaching, preaching, or praying outside of the assembled church.

7. Deaconesses were a normal ministry of the church until the late Middle Ages.

8. Women were excluded from eldership, as implied in 1 Timothy 3:11 and following.

It is not my purpose to establish whether or not a woman should speak or lead in prayer in public situations. Nor is it to argue the necessity or advisability of designating certain female servants as deaconesses. What is permissible is not necessarily expedient in every situation. Rather, my purpose is to consider whether we have applied as scriptural prohibitions certain passages which may possibly bear an alternative interpretation or may possibly have been taken out of context.

Certainly we do not want to violate clear scriptural principle; nor do we want to deny to the church the ministry of godly and capable women in a body where there is "neither Jew nor Greek, slave nor free, male nor female" (Galatians 3:28).

What is admirable about God's women in the church through the ages is their devotion and love for God shown by their perseverance. They have continued to be the very backbone of God's church, even though possibly denied some scriptural privileges and leadership positions. They have continued to keep the faith and keep the peace of the church, even though sometimes oppressed unfairly. They have shown dynamically what Paul meant when he wrote that "love perseveres."

May we honor them by restoring them to their God-given roles in his church.

Notes:

[1] The *Didache* (sometimes called the *Teachings of the Twelve Apostles*) is one of the earliest Christian documents, written shortly after the last New Testament book. It was written by an unknown author but was widely accepted in the second-century church.

[2] The Council of Orange (A.D. 441) was one of the ecumenical councils consisting of bishops, priests, and deacons which determined the doctrine of the early Catholic church.

Focusing Your Faith

1. Since you were a child how have women's roles changed in society? In church?

2. Do you think you are able to use your talents completely in the church? If not, what is holding you back?

3. How do women serve in your church?

4. After your study of this chapter, how has your attitude changed concerning women's roles in the church?

5. What matters most to God about public worship in the church?

6. Is it permissible for women to be deaconesses today? Lead singing? Lead public prayers? Teach adult classes? Preach? Teach a man? Baptize?

7. If women are to remain silent in assemblies, how can they then sing, confess sins, or even confess Jesus as Lord?

1 Corinthians 14:23

So if the whole church comes together and everyone speaks in tongues, and some who do not understand or some unbelievers come in, will they not say that you are out of your mind?

Chapter 11

Tongues

That Teach

1 Corinthians 12:1-11; 14

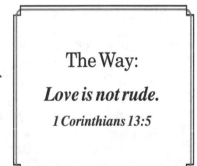

The Way:

Love is not rude.

1 Corinthians 13:5

Once when we were approaching an African village in the company of Tonga tribesmen, we heard in the distance the throbbing of the village drums. My companions stopped and listened intently, then one exclaimed, "Oh, old Kambole is dead!" I was amazed and asked, "How do you know that?" "The drums told us," they replied. "How is that possible?" I exclaimed. "They said nothing to me." "That's because you don't know their language. To us the message was perfectly clear," they said.

I'm glad the tribesmen understood the drums' message and were able to explain it to me. What a shame it would have been for the drummers to have beaten their drums in a rhythm that no one recognized. I was reminded of Paul's statement that it is pointless even to make a sound on a lifeless instrument unless it conveys something to the hearers. How much more senseless it is to use the human voice to articulate sounds in the presence of others that are meaningless to them.

Tongue Speaking

Throughout the Christian age, the phenomenon of tongue speaking (*glossolalia*) has reappeared from the latter part of the second century down to the present time. The first major movement of "neo-Pentecostalism" arose in the Montanist heresy in the last quarter of the second century. A charismatic preacher named Montanus, along with certain women disciples, began to claim the power to prophecy in "tongues." A leading church scholar of the time, Iranaeus of Lyons, dryly remarked that the difference between the tongue speaking of the apostles on Pentecost and that of Montanus and his followers was that when the apostles spoke everybody understood, and when the Montanists spoke, nobody understood.

Tongue speaking, like quaking or shaking and falling in a trance, is an expression of protest against the cold formality of empty rites and ceremonies that characterize religion when it has lost its relevancy to human needs and feelings. When the Western church made its public services nothing more than a performance by clergy in which the average member had no part except as a spectator, it was inevitable that spontaneous eruptions of pent-up feelings would occur. This happened in pre-Reformation Europe when popular evangelists began to preach to the common people. Excitement seized the audience to the degree that thousands would fall unconscious. In nineteenth-century America, audiences of Restoration preachers were sometimes seized with uncontrollable shaking. Such phenomena are often attributed to the agency of the Holy Spirit, but it should be pointed out that they occur in many religions that are not linked in any way to Christianity.

In modern times the abnormal activity attributed to a seizure by the Spirit is overwhelmingly exhibited by tongue speaking. In some groups it is so central to their faith systems that they practically equate it with being saved. Since they most often appeal to 1 Corinthians 12–14 as the doctrinal basis for their practice, it is important that we explore what the apostle Paul was really talking about when he referred to speaking in tongues.

What Was Happening in Corinth?

Paul uses the word *disorder* (or confusion) to describe a worship service at Corinth. Like naughty children, the church was more interested in showing off than they were in edifying each other or in favorably influencing visitors. Tongue speakers and

---

Like naughty children, the church was more interested in showing off than they were in edifying each other or in favorably influencing visitors.

---

prophets violated basic rules of politeness and consideration for others by constantly interrupting and speaking while others had the floor. Not to be outdone by their male counterparts, the prophetesses added to the general confusion by harassing the speaker with questions and interjections.

It was, in short, a madhouse, and Paul told them

that unbelieving visitors would draw just that very conclusion. The participants in this uproar were not simply disorganized; they were insufferably and inexcusably rude. Such rudeness could only stem from a self-serving indifference to the needs of the congregation and to the rights of each other. "Love is not rude," so we must conclude that the fundamental problem in the Corinthian church was their complete lack of love for each other as well as for the Lord.

Spiritual Gifts

Chapter 14 is a continuation of Paul's discussion of spiritual gifts which he began in chapter 12. The Corinthian Christians had received a diversity of gifts from the Holy Spirit but used them in a very selfish way for personal fulfillment or to excite the admiration of others. The apostle tries to make the "charismatics" understand their particular Spirit-endowed abilities in the context of an overall unity of purpose. Because of their misuse of the gifts to build up their own image, he addresses the root of the problem in Chapter 13—a lack of love for the body. He compares the period of miraculous gifts to the infancy of an individual. They are the "toys" of babyhood which will no longer be needed when Christians have reached maturity—a maturity they are not going to achieve until they learn to love each other.

Prophecying in Tongues

Paul begins chapter 14 by charging the Corinthians to "follow the way of love and eagerly desire spiritual gifts, especially the gift of prophecy." The Greek word for "prophecy" (*propheteia*) has nothing to do directly with foretelling the future. It might pertain to past, present, or future, but future time is not inherent in the word. It means speaking for a god. In the New Testament a prophet is a spokesperson for God. In the second century, when the charismatic gift of prophecy was no longer evident, a prophet was a traveling Christian evangelist or teacher, and the use of the word corresponds to our present term "preacher."

> *A prophet was a traveling Christian evangelist or teacher, and the use of the word corresponds to our present term "preacher."*

Paul implies that the gift of prophecy is the gift most to be desired. The Christian faith was spread by teaching the inspired Word, and there were no Bibles in the first century upon which to base such teaching. Therefore, it was of paramount importance to the growth of the kingdom that there be inspired preachers through whom the Holy Spirit could speak.

It is clear from the succeeding verse: "For anyone who speaks in a tongue does not speak to men but to God," that Paul is contrasting the relative benefit to the Corinthian church of prophecy and tongue speaking. His conclusion in verse 5: "He who prophesies is greater than one who speaks in tongues, unless he interprets, so that the church may be edified," implies that the spoken message in both cases is intended to edify the church. The difference was that the prophet's message was edifying because it was understood by the church, whereas the tongue speaker's message had to be interpreted to be edifying. In the latter case, the message spoken in a tongue was understood only by God and, obviously, the tongue speaker (since "he edifies himself").

The tongue speaker was, therefore, a prophet who was given a message in a language not his own. In verse 6, Paul stresses that a message in a tongue not understood is useless to the hearers. He illustrates this point (vv. 7, 8) by reminding them that even inanimate soundmakers like flutes, harps, and trumpets are not used to make random sounds but rather to produce a pattern of tones that communicates upon some level to the audience. In the case of the trumpet, its military usefulness is linked directly to its value in communicating instruction. In verse 9 Paul makes the application that tongues are given to communicate an understandable message, and any use of them that violates that purpose is simply speaking "into the air."

The world is filled with differing languages, but not one of them was intended for any use other than intelligible communication.

The apostle now reasons from the general to the specific. The world is filled with differing languages, but not one of them was intended for any use other than intelligible communication. "So it is with you. Unless you speak intelligible words with your tongue, how will anyone know what you are saying? You will just be speaking into the air" (v. 9).

He now asserts that there are many languages in the world, every one of which is intended to communicate. If, however, the hearer does not understand the language, speaker and hearer are foreigners to each other. Paul concludes the thought with the application, "So it is with you." The tongue speakers at Corinth were, therefore, using languages that were foreign to the Greek-speaking Corinthians, and the result was that the congregation was not edified.

Tongues in Praying

Verses 13 and 14 appear at first reading to be obscure and not directly consistent with the line of thought the apostle has been following. "For this reason anyone who speaks in a tongue should pray that he may interpret what he says. For if I pray in a tongue, my spirit prays, but my mind is unfruitful." He has already stated that the tongue speaker edifies himself (v. 4) and then proceeds to argue that a language not understood does not edify. It is therefore illogical that the tongue speaker does not himself understand what he is saying. In fact, Paul has already proposed that the tongue speaker interpret his message so that the church may be edified (v. 5).

The clear inference is that Paul is making the same application to public prayer that he has already made to public preaching. He is saying that when a tongue speaker leads a congregational prayer, he should do it in such a way that he interprets into Greek what he has said in a foreign tongue. In other words, Paul is not instructing the prayer leader to pray that the Holy Spirit may enable him to understand the meaning of his own prayer, or that the Spirit will endow him with the gift of interpretation. He is admonishing him to articulate his prayer so that he allows opportunity for it to be translated into Greek.

That he is talking about leading a prayer is made certain by verse 14: "For if I pray in a tongue." Most Bible translators have failed to translate the Greek word *nous* contextually and have rendered it "mind" instead of "meaning," which is one of the established uses of the Greek word. A better translation of

Paul's statement would be, "For if I pray in a tongue, my spirit prays, but my meaning bears no fruit." This is borne out by his practical application in verses 16 and 17. "If you are praising God with your spirit, how can one who finds himself among those who do not understand say "Amen" to your thanksgiving, since he does not know what you are saying? You may be giving thanks well enough, but the other man is not edified."

Tongues Are Languages

The NIV's use of "those who do not understand" for the Greek word *idiotos* in verse 16 is unwarranted. The New American Standard rendering "ungifted" is even less acceptable. The New English Bible (NEB) "plain man" and the Revised Standard Version (RSV) "outsider" are nearer the mark, and the KJV's "unlearned" is better still. As Arndt and Gingrich point out in their New Testament Greek lexicon, it means a "lay" person as opposed to a specialist or an uneducated person in contrast to one who has received instruction. This shows, interestingly enough, that chapter 14 is not dealing with an "unknown" or "angelic" tongue but with languages which people can be educated to speak and understand.

Chapter 14 is not dealing with an "unknown" or "angelic" tongue but with languages which people can be educated to speak and understand.

Paul asserts in verse 18 that he is linguistically gifted to a degree surpassing any of the Corinthian Christians. This certainly does not mean that he was more addicted to meaningless babble than they, but that he was empowered to speak more languages. It

might be inferred that, as an apostle, he was not
limited to a single spirit-empowered language, but
was able through the Holy Spirit to converse freely
in whatever tongue he needed to proclaim the gospel
message. It's also highly probable that as an educated person in the Judeo-Graecan world, he had
learned to speak other languages.

Whatever the case, he chose not to use a language where it was not understood. "But in the
church I would rather speak five intelligible words
[or *nous*, words with meaning] to instruct others
than ten thousand words in a tongue" (v. 19).

In verse 20 he chides the Corinthians for their
infantile use of their linguistic gifts. They were using
tongues to show off instead of using them for the
purpose for which they were given—to teach God's
Word and convert unbelievers.

In verse 21 Paul quotes Isaiah 28:11 as a prophecy foretelling the phenomenon of tongue speaking
in the New Testament age, "Through men of strange
tongues / and through the lips of foreigners / I will
speak to this people."

In Isaiah 28 the context is the rebellion and
stubbornness of Israel against heeding God's instruction. God says to them that because they are
unwilling to listen to their own Hebrew prophets, a
time will come when he will again instruct them in
languages of foreigners (Gentile tongues). Implied in
this prophecy is another age in which the Israelites,
scattered throughout the nations of the world, will
no longer be able to understand their own Hebrew
language but will have adopted Gentile tongues.
Paul's application of Isaiah 28:11 to the tongue-
speaking situation of Corinth would make no sense
if the subject under discussion is "unknown" or
"spirit" tongues.

Purpose of Tongues

In verse 21 Paul declares that the foreign languages are a sign for unbelievers, not for believers, whereas the gift of prophecy is for believers. The foreign languages were for the unsaved world; they were missionary tongues. If a missionary sent from Antioch or Corinth arrived in Iberia speaking the Iberian tongue with effortless ease, although he was obviously a new arrival on their shores, the Iberians would recognize that a miraculous event was occurring and would be constrained to accept the stranger as a messenger from God. On the other hand, a Corinthian Christian's native Greek language was the proper vehicle for edifying the Corinthian church.

The gift of tongues is a powerful evidence of divine intervention only to the unbeliever who understands the tongue.

What, then, is a possible explanation for the astonishing question in verse 23? Paul asks that if the congregation is meeting together and tongues are being employed, and a visiting person who is either uneducated or an unbeliever enters the meeting place, won't he immediately conclude that he has come into a madhouse? After having just declared that tongue speaking is a sign for the unbeliever (that is, the gift of tongues will establish the credibility of the speaker), Paul now says that the tongue speakers' credibility will be destroyed as far as the visiting stranger is concerned. How can we resolve what appears to be a glaring contradiction?

The answer is that the gift of tongues is a powerful evidence of divine intervention only to the unbeliever who understands the tongue. To one who does not understand the tongue it would be nothing more than meaningless gibberish. A Corinthian visitor would speak Greek and, unless he was well-educated, would be unlikely to understand any other language. An address from the speaker of a foreign tongue would repel rather than attract him. On the other hand, prophesying (delivering a sermon in Greek) might very well result in convicting and converting the unbeliever.

The apostle does not forbid tongue speaking in the Corinthian assembly, which may seem surprising in view of the generally negative treatment he has given the subject. In fact, he specifically instructs that the practice not be banned but rather limited to only two or three tongue speakers at a given assembly and then only if the message is interpreted. There may be two reasons why he did not forbid it outright. The first is that persons with the gift might feel slighted and irrelevant in a fellowship where all the other gifts had a valuable application. The other reason is that a demonstration of the gift before their fellow Christians might validate Paul's assertion that the Corinthians "do not lack any spiritual gift" (1 Corinthians 1:7).

Promise of Jesus

The gift of tongues was one of the promises Jesus gave to his followers: "They will speak with new tongues" (Mark 16:17). The use of the Greek word *kainos* instead of *neos* for "new" is significant. *Neos* signifies new from the standpoint of time—something that did not exist before. *Kainos* is new from the standpoint of use or user. Jesus speaks (Matthew 9:17) of pouring new (*neos*) wine into new (*kainos*) wineskins. Whereas the wine had recently come into being, the goatskins had previously existed. Their newness consisted of their being put to another use. They had formerly covered goats but were now employed in holding wine.

This promise of new tongues was dramatically fulfilled on the first Pentecost following Christ's resurrection. The apostles (some think the entire group of 120 disciples) "were filled with the Holy Spirit and began to speak in other tongues as the Spirit enabled them" (Acts 2:4). "Other tongues" in the context would obviously mean tongues other than the Aramaic these Galileans would be expected to speak. The result was that Jews present in their audience from the many far-flung communities of the Diaspora[1] were able to hear the gospel in their home languages. Some have argued that the miracle was performed upon the ears of the hearers, but that ignores the plain statement of Luke that they *spoke* in other tongues as the Spirit enabled them.

> *[Tongue speaking] was intended*
> *primarily to be an instrument of*
> *communication to the unbelieving world.*

Others have contended that the gift of tongue speaking is promised to all Christians and is even the proof of their genuine conversion. That cannot be true in view of Paul's question in 1 Corinthians 12:30: "Do all speak in tongues?" which in the context requires the answer, "Of course not."

Finally, 1 Corinthians 14 establishes that the tongue speaking at Corinth was not an ecstatic language of the spirit that was not intended to have any other purpose than the exuberance of a Spirit-filled believer. It was intended primarily to be an instrument of communication to the unbelieving world and particularly, but by no means exclusively, was a final attempt by God (Isaiah 28:11) to reclaim dispersed Israel in the languages of the Diaspora.

What Can We Conclude?

We may draw the following conclusions from this study about tongues:

1. The tongues of the New Testament age were human languages intended for teaching and communication of God's Word.

2. Tongues were all languages that could be learned.

3. Speaking in tongues was a continuing fulfillment of Jesus' promise to his immediate followers in Mark 16.

4. Tongues' purpose was the conversion of unbelievers (missionary tongues).

5. The Holy Spirit gave the gift of tongue speaking to individuals he chose, not to all Christians.

6. Tongue speaking was not a seal of one's salvation but an enabling ability, like all the charismatic gifts.

7. Tongues had very limited use in assemblies where they were not the usual language of communication.

In the church in Bangkok, Thailand, a visitor has an interesting and eye-opening experience. Bangkok, being a major metroplex of the Far East, is host to travelers from around the world. As a result, the church there is also blessed with Christians in transit. Many of those traveling brothers and sisters are English-speaking, as are the American missionaries who teach and preach in the Bangkok School of Preaching and their families. When the song leader announces a song, he announces both the Thai number and the English number. Everyone turns in his own hymn book to the appropriate page. As the singing begins, everyone is singing the exact same tune, but the Thai Christians are singing Thai words while others are singing English words. The praise is glorious, and the singers are unified in heart and message. It is the one time when language is *not* a barrier.

This combined-language singing is an all-out effort by the Thai Christians to be polite and caring to their English-speaking visitors. And that is the essence of Paul's statement that "love is not rude." Tongues are for exhorting, not for excluding others.

Notes:

[1] *Diaspora* refers to the scattering of exiled Jews into colonies outside Palestine.

Focusing Your Faith

1. How can a person know his/her spiritual gift? What is yours?

2. In today's church what gifts seem to be valued above other gifts? Which gifts build up the church (v. 12)?

3. If tongues are languages that can be learned, who do you know who might have the gift of tongues? How can it be used to glorify Christ? Could signing for the deaf be considered "a tongue"?

4. How did the disorder of the worship service in Corinth exemplify the condition of the church there?

5. The self-absorbed Corinthians loved power more than the power of love. How can you guard against that happening in your church?

6. Describe your vision of an edifying worship service. When have you experienced one like that?

7. Is it possible to speak in English but to speak in a way that others don't understand? How would Paul's instruction apply to this?

1 Corinthians 15:1-4

*Now, brothers, I want to remind you of
the gospel I preached to you, which you
received and on which you have taken your
stand. By this gospel you are saved, if you
hold firmly to the word I preached to you.
Otherwise, you have believed in vain.*

*For what I received I passed on to you as
of first importance: that Christ died for our
sins according to the Scriptures, that he
was buried, that he was raised on the third
day according to the Scriptures.*

Chapter 12

Resurrection

Reality

1 Corinthians 15

A father called his son to him and told him this story: "Once a man had three friends. The first one he loved very much, the second to a fair degree, but the third he often forgot and neglected. One day the

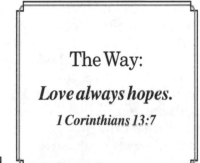

The Way:

Love always hopes.

1 Corinthians 13:7

king summoned the man to appear before him. He was alarmed at the unexpected call and looked about desperately for someone to accompany him. He begged his best friend to come, but the man replied, "There is no way that I will go with you a single step." He then pleaded with the second friend, who agreed to accompany him as far as the palace gate, but no farther. Left with no alternative, he went to the third friend and made the same request. This friend, without hesitation, assured the man that he would go with him all the way and stand beside him before the king's throne.

"Father, what has this story to do with me?" the son asked. The father replied, "It has everything to do with you, for the three friendships make up the framework of your life. The first friend is money, material wealth. He can be a good friend if he is treated wisely, but he has no loyalty and no morals. He will help you to do either good or evil. He will always be trying to gain control over you, and if he ever succeeds, he will make you his slave. He will have you completely and finally at your deathbed.

"The second friend is a person who loves you. This is a much better friend to you than the first, but he, too, has limitations. This friend will go with you to the graveside but there he will leave you, as indeed he must, for you to continue your journey alone.

"The third friend is Jesus Christ, who will meet you at the grave, take your hand in his in the resurrection, and lead you into the palace of heaven if you will only let him. All these friends are important for they affect the quality of your life. But only the third friend has the power to affect your life forever."

The Good News

Because we have a loving God who always keeps his promises, Christians are sustained by what Paul calls a "blessed hope" (Titus 2:13). How sad it is that some live out their lives "without hope and without God in the world" (Ephesians 2:12). Because we love God who loves us even more, our hope for eternal life is steadfast and unfaltering. The good news—the resurrection of Christ—confirms that hope as the vindication of a love that found its supreme expression on the cross. Because the Son of God loved us and gave himself for us, we love him in return, and that mutual love keeps our hope burning ever brighter until it is fulfilled in glory.

Without the resurrection there was nothing to preach—there was no hope.

The crucifixion is central to God's plan for our salvation. Without the death of Jesus there could have been no remission of sins. But the crucifixion, as far as human observers were concerned, was not in itself unique. The Romans crucified thousands of Jews during their administration of Palestine. The significance of what happened on the cross—the sacrifice of the Son of God for the redemption of sinners—could not be comprehended by the physical senses. What was absolutely unique was what followed the crucifixion and burial of Christ—the resurrection of a crucified body. The resurrection was the good news which was central to the proclamation of the saving message. Without the resurrection there was nothing to preach—there was no hope.

Rejection

The Jewish establishment went to elaborate pains to deflect the force of the resurrection. First, they secured the tomb to prevent it (Matthew 27:62-66). When that failed, they concocted a false story to prevent their people from believing that it had actually happened (Matthew 28:11-15). When, in spite of their precautions, the apostles began effectively to preach the resurrection, the Jewish leaders sought to contain the damage by imprisoning and threatening them (Acts 4:3, 18-21). But the message could not be stopped (4:33).

The Jewish hierarchy had a strong vested interest, both selfish and political, in discrediting Jesus as the promised Messiah (John 11:48). They knew that if the resurrection story spread among the people, then all of their efforts would be frustrated. It was not the miraculous element—that God could raise the dead to life—which they objected to. Instead, it was the personal element—that *Jesus of Nazareth* had been raised from the dead.

In the Gentile world the resurrection story was rejected by many, but for quite different reasons. The first reason was intellectual: it was contrary to all human experience—it had never been done and, therefore, could not be done. The second reason was philosophical: it would be an exercise in futility to resurrect a body from which the shade (spirit) had already departed. Because at death the spirit is freed from the body, it would make no sense to bring them together again. The Athenians were interested in Paul's message until he mentioned the resurrection, upon which some of them began to sneer (Acts 17:32).

Paul Explains the Resurrection

Paul considered the evidence of the resurrection overwhelming. Although he does not list all of Jesus' post-resurrection appearances, he lists the ones in which apostles were present. He omits the Lord's appearances to the two Marys (Matthew 28:1-10; John 20:10-18) and to the two disciples who lived at Emmaus (Luke 24:13-35). Paul's list of Jesus' appearances in 1 Corinthians 15:5-8 include those to:

1. Peter;

2. all the apostles;

3. more than 500 brethren, a majority of
   whom were still alive when he wrote
   1 Corinthians;

4. James;

5. all the apostles a second time;

6. Paul himself.

Naturally, the Lord's appearance to Paul would be the least convincing to a skeptic. He is probably referring to his experience on the road to Damascus (Acts 9:1-9). Since his companions "did not see anyone" (Acts 9:7), there was no supporting testimony. Liberal critics have expressed the view that Paul fell in a fit and had a hallucination. Nevertheless, they have to credit Paul with absolute sincerity, since he died for his conviction. But, although Paul had no supporting witness to say that *he* (Paul) had seen the Lord, there were several hundred who witnessed that *they* had seen the risen Christ. We are left, then, with a choice of accepting the resurrection or rejecting it on the basis that many of the Greeks rejected it—that it is an insult to logic to accept the testimony of more than 500 people, many of whom paid for their story with their lives. It surely is an insult to logic to accept that such a host of people would go to their deaths for a fanciful and fictitious tale.

Physical Resurrection Denials

Paul was astounded that some in the Corinthian church denied a resurrection of the dead: "But if it is preached that Christ has been raised from the dead, how can some of you say that there is no resurrection of the dead?" (1 Corinthians 15:12). These people were not directly denying the physical resurrection of

Jesus Christ or denying that there is life beyond the grave. They *were* denying that the dead bodies of departed people would be brought to life. The Greeks did not deny survival of the spirit beyond earthly life; they denied a survival of the physical body. They considered taking a physical body into a spiritual existence irrational and pointless. Paul, however, shows that these Corinthians had not considered all the ramifications of their contention:

1. If a resurrection of all the dead was impossible, then they would have to accept that Christ was not raised either. Resurrection is either possible or it isn't. You can't have it both ways.

2. If Christ was not raised, then the gospel message is nonsense.

3. If Paul preached a lie, then these Corinthians believed a fraudulent message.

4. Paul and the other apostles were liars.

5. They were not saved from their sins.

6. Christians who had already died were lost.

7. If Christianity is only an ethical system that gives no salvation, then Christians were the most pitiable people (since they were willing to suffer and die for an empty myth).

The Coming Resurrection

A physical resurrection is necessary to reverse the temporary victory of Satan. "For since death[1] came through a man, the resurrection of the dead comes also through a man. For as in Adam all die, so in Christ all will be made alive" (15:21-22). Paul is saying that physical death was completely reversed. Christ's human body was first restored as it had been. The fact that subsequently Jesus' body was able to appear inside closed rooms and to change its appearance at will is irrelevant to his argument here. When Satan tricked Adam and Eve into disobedience and they were expelled from Eden, he made them subject to mortality. They were also separated from communion with God (spiritual death), but that is not part of the argument here. In Romans 8:21-23 he explains more fully:

> The creation itself will be liberated from its bondage to decay and brought into the glorious freedom of the children of God. We know that the whole creation has been groaning as in the pains of childbirth right up to the present time. Not only so, but we ourselves, who have the firstfruits of the Spirit, groan inwardly as we wait eagerly for our adoption as sons, the redemption of our bodies.

Christians have the firstfruits of the Spirit, that is, salvation of our souls—spiritual life. We have participated in one resurrection from baptism (Ephesians 2:4-6; Revelation 20:5, 6). But Satan's work has not been completely undone. We are awaiting the rebirth of our bodies which will happen at the second resurrection. We are still subject to disease, pain, and decay. Until that is completely reversed, Christ's victory over Satan is unfinished. Our bodies must first be restored to the imperishability they had in Eden; then we will be changed into a spiritual body in a form that "has not yet been made known" (1 John 3:2). We can only wait "in eager expectation for the sons of God to be revealed" (Romans 8:19).

Stages of Resurrection

Paul explains that the physical resurrection has two parts: First Christ himself, which has already occurred. Second at his return, those who belong to Christ.[2]

Then the end will come—the end of the age and the physical universe. At that time Christ will return the kingdom to God who gave it to him after he has destroyed all power (satanic and human) that is not of God and has reigned until the last enemy (death) has been destroyed by the resurrection.

The coming resurrection, then, is the final episode of Christ's reign before he returns the kingdom to God. The resurrection occurs "when he comes." There is, therefore, no future age when Christ will reign over an earthly kingdom. The resurrection is the grand finale to all earthly existence.

Baptized for the Dead

After explaining the resurrection, Paul returns to the question he introduced in 1 Corinthians 15:12: "How can some of you say that there is no resurrection of the dead?" He continues the discussion in verse 29: "Now if there is no resurrection, what will those do who are baptized for the dead? If the dead are not raised at all, why are people [they] baptized for them?"

The question is, who are the "people"? The NIV says, "Why are people baptized for them?" "People" is an addition in the NIV; "they" is the correct subject. The *they* (people) of verse 29 must have the logical antecedent: *some of you* (who said there was no resurrection) of verse 12. To use a common illustration: It would make no sense to ask, "If Tom prefers Volkswagons, why does John drive a Ford?" Consistency requires the same subject in the first clause as in the second clause. The construction would require the form, "If Tom prefers Volkswagons, why does *he* (Tom) drive a Ford?"

Some of the Corinthian Christians were denying the resurrection. In 1 Corinthians 15:29 Paul is pointing out their inconsistency, "Now if there is no resurrection, . . . " meaning, If our arguments for a resurrection are not true, . . . "What are they doing being baptized for the dead?" meaning, Why go through a ritual that is for the dead? ty.

Since even those Corinthian Christians who denied the possibility of a resurrection were themselves baptized, what could they possibly have been baptized for? The entire Christian faith is based upon just such a resurrection of the dead. Even in baptizm we re-enact the death, burial, and resurrection of Christ. It is the act of faith by which we are separated from the deadness of our former lives and are raised new creatures (Romans 6:3, 4). It makes the sacrifice of Jesus Christ effective in redeeming our souls. His blood removes past, present, and future sins (1 John 1:7). Certainly baptism does not bring any tangible benefits during earthly life. Its entire purpose, then, must relate to an expectation beyond this life, that is, after death. It does nothing for the living but holds a rich promise for the dead.

False Assumptions

Failure to interpret this passage within the context of the immediate problem introduced and discussed in 1 Corinthians 15:12-58 has led to many false conclusions based on verse 29. Some have incorrectly assumed that this verse is referring to vicarious baptism for dead relatives and friends who were not baptized during their earthly life. Among those misinterpretations of this passage are that groups such as some first-century mystery religions, heretical Christian groups among the Gentiles, and some members of the Corinthian church were, rightly or wrongly, engaged in this practice, and that vicarious baptism was considered a valid and recognized practice of the early church. All of these conclusions share the fatal objection that they do not relate to the context.

Christians are not baptized for the living, but for the **dead**—*on behalf of a future time when their own dead bodies will be raised to immortality.*

An assumption that Paul is referring to baptism on behalf of unidentified persons already dead is unwarranted. Such a practice was otherwise unknown in the New Testament church, and Paul does not challenge it as being in any way heretical. What members of the mystery cults or heretical Christian groups practiced would have no bearing whatsoever on Paul's argument of inconsistency against "some of you" Corinthian Christians. The objects of his argument, therefore, must be those denying a resurrection but practicing baptism. Paul is saying, in other words, that Christians are not baptized for the living, but for the *dead*—on behalf of a future time when their own dead bodies will be raised to immortality.

Martyrs for Christ

In verse 30 Paul returns to his original argument developed in verses 14-19 that the hazardous choice of being an active first-century Christian made no sense if the resurrection is untrue: "Why do we endanger ourselves every hour? I die every day—I mean that, brothers—." The apostles were a prime target for the church's enemies because they gave personal testimony of Christ's resurrection. They expected to be martyred sooner or later. So every day when they went out to preach was very possibly their last day on earth.

Paul added that he certainly would never have fought "wild beasts" in Ephesus for any human reason. Whether he is referring to the Ephesian mob as "wild beasts" (Acts 19) or to an actual arena struggle with wild animals is not certain. He quotes Isaiah 22:13 in bitter irony: "Let us eat and drink, for tomorrow we die." He is not recommending that course of life; he simply means, "We might as well do that as preach if it's all for nothing anyway."

Life After Death

Some of the Greeks had decided against the idea of a bodily resurrection on the grounds that the human body was created for earthly life and would not suit a different dimension of existence. For instance, they asked if the dead would be raised with their sexual differences, even though Jesus said in the resurrection there would be no marriage. Paul responds in essence: "That is silly! God has created an infinite number of life forms. Don't you suppose that he has already determined what he is going to make us like?"

In general terms, we will have a different body in many respects. That naturally follows from our dual being. Our body is descended from Adam, but the second Adam (Christ) is the source of our spiritual life. An earthly being cannot be the same as a heavenly being. As we have been born in the image of Adam, we will be reborn in the resurrection in the heavenly image of Christ. Our body will not be perishable but imperishable. At death it will be buried in dishonor (meaning that it is temporarily defeated by death), but in the resurrection it will be raised a glorious body. It is sown in weakness; it will be raised in power. It is buried a physical body; it will be raised a spiritual body (1 Corinthians 15:42-44).

Of course, we can never understand with our human limitations what life in a fully spiritual dimension will be like. We can understand the unknown only in comparison to the known—what we know by experience. Paul had been given a glimpse into the heavenly existence, but what he heard could not be expressed and what he saw could not be described.[3] It would be like trying to explain computer technology to a primitive Indian of the Amazon jungles. After all our imaginative concepts of the heavenly existence and the superlative preachers have used to describe it, we, like the Queen of Sheba, shall no doubt exclaim when we actually experience it: "Not even half was told me."

What Does the Resurrection Mean?

Alexander Campbell was once walking through a meadow with Robert Owen, the atheist. Owen, who was currently engaged in a series of discussions with Campbell on the validity of Christian theism, remarked, "I have no fear of death." "But," Campbell pressed him, "do you have any hope in death?" "None," Owen replied. "Then," Campbell stated, "you are no different from that cow grazing over there. She has no fear of death either, but neither does she have any hope."

To Paul, as indeed to all New Testament preachers, there was no message to preach unless the bodily resurrection of Jesus was an established fact—and this is equally true today. If we deny or discount the resurrection (through our words, our thoughts, or our actions), we are left only with a superior system of ethics which, though valuable, is hardly worth dying for. But Jesus' resurrection has awesome implications for the one who accepts it. It means that

- Jesus of Nazareth was, in truth, the Son of God;

- each of us will also be raised from the dead;

- each of us will stand before a final judgment to be judged by the One who was first raised from the dead (Acts 17:31).

But it also means that

- I cannot simply live my life without God's being the prime factor, because nothing physical or time-related has any real importance except as it relates to eternity;

- I can have the assurance of my salvation;

- I have an abiding responsibility to share the message of hope with others to whom the resurrection is not yet real.

The resurrection is a fact. And it's the whole basis for our continuing hope of heaven. It's more than a hope that wishes; it's a hope that trusts. Without it we have no hope whatsoever beyond this paltry earthly existence. God's love in raising Jesus from death so that we might be raised later to eternal life is overwhelming. "It is by this gospel that you are saved" (15:2). When we realize that it is this simple good news of the resurrection that makes all the difference, all the noise and confusion of our daily lives and our "church work" seem so insignificant. When we put our emphasis on loving Christ and others, we respond to his phenomenal gift, and our "love always hopes."

Notes:

[1] Paul is discussing physical death here. This passage is not a parallel with Romans 5:12 where spiritual death is meant. Moulton and Milligan, *Vocabulary of the Greek Testament,* p. 451.

[2] The resurrection of the wicked to eternal death is not within the scope of Paul's subject here.

[3] The Greek translation of *ouk exon* as "not permitted" in 2 Corinthians 12:4 misses the point. Paul is saying: "it is *not possible*" to describe it.

Focusing Your Faith

1. Whose death has been the hardest for you to deal with? What did you learn through the experience?

2. What does it mean to say, "Christians are not baptized for the living but for the dead"?

3. As you contemplate your own death, what comforts you most? What do you fear most?

4. How can your church help families facing death in your community?

5. What do you look forward to most about your new resurrected body? Your spiritual body?

6. If you were to explain our resurrection from death to a friend who doesn't know the good news, what would you say?

7. Can you successfully share the good news of Christ if you are not totally sure of your own salvation?

1 Corinthians 12:31b; 13:13

And now I will show you the most excellent way.

And now these three remain: faith, hope and love. But the greatest of these is love.

Chapter 13

The Most
Excellent Way

1 Corinthians 13

Andondile is a grandfather now, but I will always remember him as he was when he came to us.

Andondile was twelve when I first saw him, a tiny little black boy shivering on the

> # The Way:
>
> *But the greatest of these is love.*
>
> *1 Corinthians 13:13*

doorstep in the cold gray dawn of an African mountain winter. He was blind in one eye, and a tattered old piece of cloth which served as his garment did not hide his thin chest or his spindly arms and legs. He looked as though he had never in his whole life had one good meal, and he probably hadn't. But the thing that struck me most forcefully was his face—the indomitable spirit that blazed from his one good eye and the resolute firmness of his small chin. It was the face of a little boy grown old, his childhood lost forever in some twilight of struggle through which he had come. It was a face which had learned sorrow without bitterness, and suffering without despair, and somehow it conveyed the quiet serenity of a spirit that has withstood life's hardest blows and knows that nothing worse can come.

And now he stood there in the biting chill and looked me firmly in the eye, but his childish lips trembled as he asked for a job. Long later he told me that as he faced me, he turned sick with fear, but on that morning I never suspected that his courage wavered. I could see only that this determined little mite intended to work for me, and so Andondile became a part of our life.

In the ensuing months, he became indispensable. Nothing that needed doing ever escaped his notice. If a stray donkey got into the corn, he saw it first; and if a pig was lost, it was Andondile who brought it back before anyone else knew it was gone. Through the long dry months he lugged five-gallon cans of water up from the spring to keep the flowers alive, and when the torrential rains of summer kept the other workers in their huts, we could always depend upon him to appear for work. He did his work with a fierce intensity which was almost frightening, for we did not know the dreams that lit the breast of this little boy.

One day Andondile stood at the door, and it was clear that his visit was of unusual significance, because he had suddenly developed a nervous cough and his toes were wriggling in a fit of embarrassment. Finally it came out. He wanted to go with us on a trip to the town of Mbeya for supplies.

He had never seen a town, and there was stardust in his eye on that afternoon when we drove into the drab, dusty little trading post which supplied this part of the African bush with sugar, flour, and mosquito nets. I was curious to see how Andondile was going to squander his accumulated wages amidst all the temptations and glamour of soccer balls, sugar sticks, and soda pop. He came back to the car lugging a large bundle, and he walked with the pride of a prince of the realm. His face was shining, and he undid the coarse string and heavy brown paper with loving fingers as one might unveil a Rembrandt. Inside were two cheap, yellow cotton blankets. Taken aback, I asked, "What did you get them for, Andondile?" "The babies were crying with the cold," he replied simply.

After this, I determined to dig up the background of this little boy who was so untypical of most of the children I have known. I found that he was the oldest of four children of a widow. The father had died of pneumonia two years before. With a baby and two other small children, the mother was hardly able to dig and plant their small field of corn and potatoes. Upon Andondile's small shoulders and great heart had fallen the responsibility of providing for his family of five. Now I understood why he worked as if life itself depended upon him—it did.

We began trying to help in small ways, but if ever it smacked of charity, Andondile let us know po-litely, but firmly, that he could provide for his own. On the other hand, Andondile was always happy for a chance to earn extra money. Once after he had amassed considerable extra time, his overtime pay came to five shillings. He smiled happily as he took it and said, "Now the babies can have some sugar in their porridge."

A few months after the "babies" had gotten their blankets, he bought a still finer blanket for his mother. And the day he brought home a piece of calico for her new dress, he almost burst with pride. Up until this time he had no blanket for himself, and he still slept curled up by the hut fire in his clothes until he awakened cramped and stiff from cold and added sticks to the dying embers. I decided it was time to meddle. "Andondile," I said sternly, "I am taking twenty shillings to buy you a blanket. I will deduct it from your wages at the rate of five shillings a month." He gravely nodded his head in agreement, but he looked troubled, and I think he felt he was letting his family down in taking money from the "babies" and his mother and using it for himself.

By Western standards of culture, Andondile was a savage. He ate white ants, scooping them into his mouth with his hand, and if he had been given a fork he would have used it for combing his hair. He believed in witchcraft and black magic. The deeper implications of intellectual and moral refinement held no meaning for him. Yet he understood the very essence of love.

Andondile had learned more from life and given more to enrich the lives of others than many whose portraits hang in halls of fame. He reaffirmed my belief in the innate nobility of the human soul, as God made it in the beginning, without regard to color, race, or tongue. He helped me to recapture a belief in the constancy of love, which will one day stand forth in eternal clarity when all earthly things have vanished into the mists of yesterday.

Back to Basics

Andondile's family was all-important to him. He did nothing for himself, and did everything for his family. The church could take a lesson from Andondile's selfless example.

Paul wrote chapter 13 of 1 Corinthians to selfish,

immature Christians. Their rivalry and striving for position had made their church family dysfunctional. Their praise services had become a bickering madhouse; the Lord's Supper had become a farce. Deep divisions fragmented their fellowship, and there was no order nor community of purpose. Like children, the Corinthians were disputing over the relative superiority of the various charismatic gifts. They were ignoring the fact that they were all part of the same body—the body of Christ, the church.

Paul wanted them to understand that love is greater than any spiritual gift and even greater than faith and hope. So, after he reprimands the Corinthians for their various acts of misbehavior, Paul gently introduces chapter 13: "And now I will show you the most excellent way." He lovingly talks to the Corinthian church about love—the solution to their problems.

What Is Love?

The word for love that is most frequently used in the New Testament is *agape*. It is for all practical purposes a "Christian" word. It occurs occasionally in classical Greek but without the same content of meaning. The ancient Greeks used it to mean keen enthusiasm, especially for sports. Possibly under the influence of the Old Testament word for love (*ahabah* in Hebrew) and the need for a Greek equivalent for translating both the Old Testament text and the Aramaic preaching of Jesus, *agape* became the word of choice. *Agape* is primarily a love of the will, to desire another's good and to willingly seek another's good.

The other Greek words that express some different meanings of the English word love are *philia* (emotional love, friendship) and *eros* (romantic or

sexual love). *Philia* occurs a number of times in the
Greek testament, but *eros* is not used.

The English word *love* is somewhat ambiguous
and is used for a number of concepts with widely
varying connotations. That is, no doubt, why the
King James translators used the word *charity* to
translate *agape* in 1 Corinthians 13. *Charity* derives
from the Greek word *charis* (grace or graciousness)
and in the seventeenth century when the KJV was
translated, *charity* satisfactorily translated *agape*,
but no more. Through the centuries it has acquired a
cold, impersonal aloofness of mechanical benevolence that no longer conveys the heartfelt compul-
sion to become involved in promoting the welfare of
others that it once did. As a matter of fact, a common
expression to indicate the severity of winter's chill is:
"It is as cold as charity." There is no remote detach-
ment in *agape*; it is the most involved word in the
New Testament.

The Greatest of These

In Romans 5:1, 2, 5, Paul says, "Therefore, since
we have been justified through faith, we have peace
with God through our Lord Jesus Christ, through
whom we have gained access by faith into this grace
in which we now stand. And we rejoice in the hope of
the glory of God. And hope does not disappoint us,
because God has poured out his love into our hearts
by the Holy Spirit, whom he has given us." In this
explanation, Paul has moved from faith to hope to
love. All three are beautiful words, and each is an
essential ingredient in the Christian's relationship
to God. By placing love at the pinnacle, Paul implies
a greater content of meaning than the casual reader
might surmise. To understand this emphasis on love,

we must first consider faith and hope.

Faith

It is difficult to imagine a quality surpassing faith, especially since the whole Christian system is, from the human standpoint, a relationship of faith. "For it is by grace you have been saved, through faith" (Ephesians 2:8). The book of Hebrews defines faith in eloquent terms: "Now faith is being sure of what we hope for and certain of what we do not see" (Hebrews 11:1). Then it gives an honor roll of great heroes of the faith—people who served their generation well and earned a place in salvation history because they were filled with faith. Abraham is particularly commended because he believed what was manifestly impossible. "Without faith it is impossible to please God, because anyone who comes to him must believe that he exists and that he rewards those who earnestly seek him" (Hebrews 11:6).

Without the faith of one man, humanity would have been wiped off the planet. Noah believed against all experience and reason and against the collective judgment of all his neighbors that God would destroy the world with water. So he set about the long, arduous task of collecting enough cypress wood to build a large ocean liner and then undertook the daunting toil of actually building it.

Jesus said faith as small as a mustard seed was strong enough to move a mountain (Matthew 17:20). Christians are able to stand in a saved relationship to God through Christ by their faith (Romans 11:20). The righteousness which grace bestows upon the redeemed sinner is obtained on the basis of faith "from first to last" (Romans 1:17).

The faith of Christians of the first three centuries

in withstanding the onslaught of the Roman Empire is proverbial. Their faith gave them hope. Their steadfast trust in God empowered them to face wild beasts or even burning at the stake without denying their faith in Christ. Quite clearly, faith ennobles us and enables us to be much more than we would otherwise have the potential to become. If love is greater than faith, then it surely must be dynamite!

Hope

Hope is also a magnificent concept. Without hope we are only intelligent animals without any purpose beyond the present existence. Hope transcends present reality and lays claim to what can be. It enables us to reach above the mundane and commonplace and dream of immortality. Paul says, "We rejoice in the hope of the glory of God" (Romans 5:2). Hope enables humans (like God) to see "the things that are not" (1 Corinthians 1:28).

If love is greater than faith,
then it surely must be dynamite!

Hope makes our mortality acceptable because it sees beyond death to our permanent home. It gives us an incalculably great advantage over those who are without hope because we can ask with Hosea: "Where, O death, are your plagues? Where, O grave, is your destruction?" (13:14). Because of hope, the Christian does not "grieve like the rest of men, who have no hope" (1 Thessalonians 4:13).

Hope is the mainstay of the suffering Christian, a precious gift from God. "Remember your word to your servant, / for you have given me hope. / My comfort in my suffering is this: / Your promise preserves my life" (Psalm 119:49, 50). The reason

Christians are able to endure persecution and even martyrdom is their abiding hope. The Thessalonians were able to bear mistreatment because of their "endurance inspired by hope in our Lord Jesus Christ" (1 Thessalonians 1:3). Paul defended himself for his adversarial relationship to the Jews before King Agrippa by saying: "It is because of my hope in what God has promised our fathers that I am on trial today" (Acts 26:6).

Hope truly gives man a new perspective on life and its problems. It makes the struggle well worthwhile. It was in the confidence of hope that Paul was able to write: "I consider that our present sufferings are not worth comparing with the glory that will be revealed in us" (Romans 8:18). If hope can inspire men to such heights of dedication that they will gladly sacrifice their lives for it, then it is difficult to conceive of any greater quality than that. And yet, Paul says that love is greater still.

Love

Love has one aspect that makes it a nobler virtue than faith and hope. While all three are focused upon something outside the individual, faith and hope ultimately reflect back to the benefit of that individual. I have faith that through Jesus Christ I will ultimately receive eternal life, and my hope is centered upon that promised reward. But love is focused upon something outside of myself—upon seeking another's good. When we are able to truly love even an enemy, then we come closest to knowing the very nature of God himself, for God is love (1 John 4:8).

Characteristics of Love

In 1 Corinthians 13:4-7 Paul analyzes the

primary characteristics of real love:

1. Love is patient. Because God is patient, he bears with our faults so that we may eventually be saved (2 Peter 3:9). Patience is a fruit of the Spirit (Galatians 5:22) and is necessary in order to inherit the promised reward (Hebrews 6:12).

2. Love is kind. Kindness is the response of a tender, concerned heart. Jesus said love even for enemies should characterize his disciples. When we do good to them we will really be "sons of the Most High" who is kind even to the ungrateful and wicked (Luke 6:35). How much more should we be kind to those with whom we expect to spend eternity. Paul wrote to the Ephesians: "Be kind and compassionate to one another, forgiving each other, just as in Christ God forgave you" (Ephesians 4:32).

3. Love does not envy. Proverbs 14:30 says "envy rots the bones." It is like a malignant tumor that eats away at contentment until the heart that harbors it knows no peace. Envy led King Ahab to vicious murder and eventually to his own violent death (1 Kings 21 and 22). Envy of their brother Joseph drove Jacob's sons to sell him into slavery. Envy of anyone else's good fortune or achievements quickly leads to hatred of that person.

4. Love does not boast. Evildoers boast of themselves (Psalm 94:4), but the godly boast in the Lord (Psalm 34:2). Those who love worldly things rather than God are arrogant and boastful (2 Timothy 3:2-4). A Christian knows that he owes what he is to God's grace and that he has no occasion to boast (Ephesians 2:8-10). We cannot genuinely love God and our neighbor if we are boastful.

5. Love is not proud. The wicked wear their pride like a necklace (Psalm 73:6). One of the reasons God destroyed the Moabites was their excessive pride (Jeremiah 48:29). Pride leads people to worship false gods (Psalm 40:4). Although the context of the fortieth Psalm suggests literal idolatry, people today are also led by pride to serve the altars of many false gods: power, wealth, and popularity.

6. *Love is not rude.* Rudeness shows a lack of sensitivity for the feelings of others. It is completely self-centered and indifferent to the devastation that a cruel remark can wreak upon the dignity of another. Even the social world, without recourse to spiritual values, considers rudeness intolerable. It is altogether incompatible with love.

7. *Love is not self-seeking.* As Jesus pointed out, doing favors for others in order to receive favors in return is characteristic of sinners, not of Christians (Luke 6:33). Genuine love gives to others even when there is no prospect of their reciprocating.

8. *Love is not easily angered.* A leader of God's people must not be quick-tempered (Titus 1:7), but every Christian is exhorted to get rid of anger (Ephesians 4:31). Even though anger is a natural response to extreme provocation, the child of God must not foster or nurture it (Ephesians 4:26); otherwise it will lead to sin.

9. *Love keeps no record of wrongs.* It is a wonderful quality of love that it does not harbor grudges. When we consider that God has completely and for all time forgiven us, we have no choice but to forgive each other (Ephesians 4:32; Colossians 3:13). There must be no limit to a Christian's capacity for forgiveness (Matthew 18:21, 22).

10. *Love does not delight in evil but rejoices in truth.* Love wants the best possible for every human being, both for this life and for eternity. It grieves when error prevails and is joyful when error is

overcome by truth.

11. Love protects, trusts, hopes, perseveres. Love is constructive in every situation. It never gives up and never turns its back upon need. It believes the best about everyone and extends itself to make the best come true.

Love Is the Bond of Perfection

"Love never fails. But where there are prophecies, they will cease; where there are tongues, they will be stilled; where there is knowledge, it will pass away. For we know in part and we prophesy in part, but when perfection comes, the imperfect disappears" (1 Corinthians 13: 8-10).

Paul is emphasizing the relative unimportance of temporary things when compared to things that will last. The Corinthians were obsessed with charismatic gifts. The apostle tells them that these special abilities given by the Spirit are simply necessary helps until the church becomes a fully-functioning viable entity. He lists three: prophecy, tongues, and (inspired) knowledge given to some for the benefit of all for the entire roster of Spirit-endowed gifts.

"When perfection comes, the imperfect disappears." This statement has given rise to much speculation as to what *perfection* (literally, the complete or mature) refers to. Among views that have been expressed are

- the perfect state of the saints—heaven;
- the coming of Jesus Christ, the perfect one;
- the New Testament, the perfect law of liberty (based on James 1:25).

None of these fit the context. Grammatically, heaven would be possible, but the use of the neuter gender in the passage rules out both *Jesus Christ* and *law*, both of which are masculine. There is no antecedent of *"the* perfect thing" anywhere in the passage, and so the laws of Greek exegesis dictate that a neuter gender adjective or pronoun without an antecedent demands that it refer to the immediate context, as in Ephesians 2:8, where "the gift of God" cannot refer to either *grace* or *faith* and therefore must refer to the subject being discussed, which is *salvation*. Paul sets the context in the comparison of his own infancy (characterized by playing with toys, etc.) and his subsequent maturity (marked by putting his childish ways behind him). This is a parallel passage to Ephesians 4:7-13 where the identical word translated "perfection" (NIV) in 1 Corinthians 13:10, is translated "mature" in Ephesians 4:13.

The apostle is developing the theme that, until they have learned to love one another, the Corinthians will never be able to use the charismatic gifts to fulfill their purpose of a temporary scaffolding in building up a mature church that will no longer require the help of special miraculous gifts. Love is indeed "the bond of perfection" (Colossians 3:14, KJV).

The Most Excellent Way

Paul's prayer for the Ephesian church could have been written for the Corinthian church—and today's church as well:

For this reason I kneel before the Father, from whom his whole family in heaven and on earth derives its name. I pray that out of his glorious riches he may strengthen you with power through his Spirit in your inner being, so that Christ may dwell in your hearts through faith. And I pray that you, being rooted and established in love, may have power, together with all the saints, to grasp how wide and long and high and deep is the love of Christ, and to know this love that surpasses knowledge—that you may be filled to the measure of all the fullness of God (Ephesians 3:14-19).

In order to be filled with the fullness of God, Christians must keep growing and maturing. How do we know when we've reached spiritual maturity? Paul tells us in Ephesians 4:14-16:

Then we will no longer be infants, tossed back and forth by the waves, and blown here and there by every wind of teaching and by the cunning and craftiness of men in their deceitful scheming. Instead, speaking the truth in love, we will in all things grow up into him who is the Head, that is, Christ. From him the whole body, joined and held together by every supporting ligament, grows and builds itself up in love, as each part does its work.

The Corinthians had a long way to go to achieve maturity. So do we today. Only when we are able to stand firm in truth which is rooted in love will we be able to work together to build up Christ's body—the church. By heeding Paul's message of love, we can learn to follow the most excellent way.

The oil lamp was flickering and low. The warm orange rays of sunset had turned to a cool silver shimmer across the Asiatic Sea, and a gentle breeze stirred the curtain at Paul's window.

Rubbing his weary eyes and raking his work-worn hand through thinning hair, the apostle added the final words to his letter:

"I, Paul, write this greeting in my own hand.

"If anyone does not love the Lord—a curse be on him. Come, O Lord!

"The grace of the Lord Jesus be with you. My love to all of you in Christ Jesus. Amen."

Laying aside the old quill pen, Paul waited for the final words of the letter to dry. Then he carefully rolled the parchment up, tied it with a ribbon, and sealed it with his hot wax seal. He would take it down to the ship bound for Corinth at dawn. It was urgent that his message reach them right away.

Tired from his night's heart-wrenching work, Paul stretched and walked outside. He strolled down to the beach and wearily sat down on an old driftwood log where he relaxed, listening to the rhythm of the sea quietly lapping against the sand and staring at the blazing stars of heaven. He felt the very presence of God, and the thought came to him, "Love is the heartbeat of the universe. It binds us to God's eternal purpose for our existence, and is the sure foundation of our eternal future. It is the most powerful force in time or eternity, and the most enduring.

Paul got up and started back to his room. As he closed the door, he reflected and said aloud to himself, "When stars and galaxies have passed forever into the mists of yesterday, love will go on forever, resplendent and untarnished."

Focusing Your Faith

1. What, in your opinion, is the greatest love song of all time? What key words come to your mind?

2. What would make good works, faith, and even martyrdom worthless?

3. Which characteristic of love is the easiest for you to show? The most difficult?

4. Think of a way you can show love this week to that difficult person in your life. Which characteristic of love will you focus on?

5. How is love the bond of perfection (v. 10)?

6. What does Paul mean when he tells the Corinthians about "the most excellent way"?

7. On a maturity scale of 1 to 10, based on its ability to love, how would your congregation rate? How would you rate?